Guardians of Thought

Limits on Freedom of Expression in Iran

August 1993

A Middle East Watch Report

Human Rights Watch

New York • Washington • Los Angeles • London

Printed in the United States of America.

Library of Congress Card Catalog Number: 93-78899
ISBN: 1-56432-106-1

Middle East Watch

Middle East Watch was founded in 1989 to establish and promote observance of internationally recognized human rights in the Middle East. The chair of Middle East Watch is Gary Sick and the vice chairs are Lisa Anderson and Bruce Rabb. Andrew Whitley is the executive director; Eric Goldstein is the research director; Virginia N. Sherry and Aziz Abu Hamad are associate directors; Suzanne Howard is the associate.

HUMAN RIGHTS WATCH

Human Rights Watch conducts regular, systematic investigations of human rights abuses in some sixty countries around the world. It addresses the human rights practices of governments of all political stripes, of all geopolitical alignments, and of all ethnic and religious persuasions. In internal wars it documents violations by both governments and rebel groups. Human Rights Watch defends freedom of thought and expression, due process of law and equal protection of the law; it documents and denounces murders, disappearances, torture, arbitrary imprisonment, exile, censorship and other abuses of internationally recognized human rights.

Human Rights Watch began in 1978 with the founding of Helsinki Watch by a group of publishers, lawyers and other activists and now maintains offices in New York, Washington, D.C., Los Angeles, London, Moscow, Belgrade, Zagreb and Hong Kong. Today, it includes Africa Watch, Americas Watch, Asia Watch, Helsinki Watch, Middle East Watch, the Fund for Free Expression and three collaborative projects, the Arms Project, Prison Project and Women's Rights Project. Human Rights Watch is an independent, nongovernmental organization, supported by contributions from private individuals and foundations. It accepts no government funds, directly or indirectly.

Addresses for Human Rights Watch

485 Fifth Avenue
New York, NY 10017-6104
Tel: (212) 972-8400
Fax: (212) 972-0905

1522 K Street, N.W., #910
Washington, DC 20005
Tel: (202) 371-6592
Fax: (202) 371-0124

10951 West Pico Blvd., #203
Los Angeles, CA 90064
Tel: (310) 475-3070
Fax: (310) 475-5613

90 Borough High Street
London, UK SE1 1LL
Tel: (071) 378-8008
Fax: (071) 378-8029

ARDESHIR

TABLE OF CONTENTS

Acknowledgments

The information presented in this report is based on interviews conducted between January and July 1993 by Middle East Watch staff and persons familiar with the events discussed. Out of concern for their well-being, as reprisals against those who criticize the Islamic Republic are commonplace, the names of many interviewees are not disclosed.

We wish to extend our gratitude to all the persons whose cooperation and information made this report possible.

This report was written by Sarvenaz Bahar, an attorney and Sophie Silberberg Fellow with Human Rights Watch. It was edited by Human Rights Watch consultant, Cynthia Brown. Andrew Whitley, executive director of Middle East Watch, and Gara LaMarche, executive director of the Fund for Free Expression, offered suggestions on the text.

Linda Long, associate of Human Rights Watch, prepared this manuscript for publication.

We are grateful for the two drawings portrayed in this report, gifts from Iranian cartoonist and illustrator Ardeshir Mohassess.

INTRODUCTION

Now look at the number of newspapers and magazines that are currently being published in Iran. What country has so many newspapers and magazines? And they write whatever they wish.

--Supreme Religious Leader
Ayatollah Ali Khamenei
February 1993[1]

We are not opposed to the cinema, to radio, or to television; what we oppose is vice and the use of media to keep our young people in a state of backwardness and dissipate their energies.

--Late Supreme Religious Leader
Ayatollah Ruhollah Khomeini
February 1979[2]

The apparent intensity of public debate, variety of publications and the wealth of artistic achievements in the Islamic Republic of Iran create an illusion of unrestricted discourse. But the limits of expression are defined in complex and often arbitrary ways by a government beset by internal power struggles and intolerance. The artistic and intellectual community's resistance to state-imposed censorship has produced some relaxation of control since the early 1980s. But the parameters of what is permitted tend to shift quickly, in response to pressures within the ruling movement. It is never clear whether what can be said, written or filmed today will be cause for financial ruin, arrest or other punishment tomorrow.

The large-scale purges of academics and killings of dissidents, including writers, journalists and artists, that characterized the years

---

[1] Tehran Voice of the Islamic Republic of Iran, February 1993, as reported in Foreign Broadcast Information Service, *Near East and South Asia Daily Report* [hereinafter FBIS], February 8, 1993.

[2] Ruhollah Khomeini, *Islam and Revolution: Writings and Declarations* (London: KPI Limited, 1985) (Hamid Algar trans.), p. 254.

following the 1979 revolution have not continued. Public debate has become somewhat more free and publications somewhat more various in recent years. Many of the government's domestic and foreign policies are criticized in newspapers, although only by fellow partisans of the ruling movement. In some arenas, notably film, artistic achievement in the past decade has been astounding.

Despite these improvements, however, the limits of discourse are strictly defined, and the range of speakers is limited to the various factions of the ruling elite. There are no independent newspapers. Books and films are issued a release permit only after passing a rigorous process of political vetting. The moral character of magazine editors must be approved by the government, and every issue of a magazine must be submitted to the Ministry of Culture and Islamic Guidance after publication. Magazines are generally precluded from covering political issues and offering overt social criticism. In the case of "undesirable" stories, the magazine risks official closure, and its staff can face imprisonment and prosecution. Journalists are generally considered a suspect group and have the minimum of job security. They are restricted by forbidden realms of news -- until such time as that news filters in through foreign broadcasts and publications. Artists and intellectuals run the risks of personal ruin, censorship or banning, and detention.

Laws are applied selectively and inconsistently, and there is uncertainty as to the governing norms. Hard-sought government permits provide no guarantee for the continued existence and distribution of the work approved or the protection of the artist or intellectual involved. The criticism of influential pressure groups can become an extrajudicial "public prosecution" of the artist or intellectual; on the other hand, legal prosecution is often conducted in disregard of the legal provisions and guarantees of domestic law. The accused are indicted under broad and all-encompassing charges such as "moral corruption," "anti-revolutionary behavior" and "siding with global arrogance."

The ineffectiveness of the legal system is combined with an element of anarchy, which directly threatens the artistic and intellectual community. Gangs of motorcycle riders or other vigilantes trash magazine offices and publishing houses and threaten lives as self-proclaimed enforcers of the law, in the name of protecting Islamic values. This they do with the evident tolerance of the authorities, without fear of prosecution. Vilification campaigns orchestrated by the state-affiliated press commonly assign intellectuals and artists such labels as submissive servant of imperialism, activist of Communism, panegyrist of the Pahlavi regime and agent of SAVAK, the deposed Shah's secret police.

The ebbs and flows of control and censorship, however, reflect interfactional conflicts. Forms of expression in Iran, whether book, film or a woman's head cover, are invested with political significance; they may signal a loosening of control and increased tolerance of diverse views and values, or the converse. In striking at an author or film director, political factions aim at each other in their perpetual struggle for political power. Film director Mohsen Makhmalbaf, in a letter to the state-affiliated press regarding its "public prosecution" of him and his work, stated:

> The writer of these columns knows well that these arguments have nothing to do with him. The fight is over nothing other than the struggles between the different factions who seek power.[3]

Subsequent to the "public prosecution," his work was banned.

In this report, which covers primarily the period 1989-1993, Middle East Watch examines the various mechanisms of state control of expression and presents more than sixty individual cases (and one group case involving 162 persons) of Iranian writers, filmmakers, journalists and intellectuals who have been imprisoned, prosecuted or otherwise punished for the content of their work or whose work has been banned and censored. The breadth of censorship goes well beyond the cases examined here; these only serve to illustrate tactics of direct and often violent pressure by vigilante groups, of vilification campaigns, of formal censorship, and of the power play between different pressure groups within the ruling elite. The report's focus is on artistic and journalistic expression, but we also include material on some well-known cases of suppressed political expression. Also included are general assessments of the academic environment and Iranian cultural heritage.

Our analysis of mechanisms of state control includes nominally non-governmental pressure groups and entities, such as foundations and newspapers. Power struggles within Iran's ruling elite and the lack of centralized authority mean that elements as diverse as semi-autonomous

---

[3] *Film* (Iran), March 1991, p. 125.

foundations led by influential clergy[4] and state-affiliated newspapers aligned with different political factions[5] play a pivotal role in defining how journalists, writers and artists may express themselves on issues of personal and political importance. The government's role in institutionalizing control and censorship ranges from the deliberate unleashing of the more uncompromising pressure groups to taking shelter behind a real or purported inability to counter their force and will.

The Iranians whose cases are described in this report have little organized support in their home country, yet most of them continue to speak out. The relaxation of censorship during Minister of Culture and Islamic Guidance Mohammad Khatami's tenure (1989-1992) was largely their doing, the product of their persistent and often lonely protests. Since Khatami's resignation, however, even those small gains are newly endangered. The marks of his more conservative successor, Ali Larijani, a former deputy minister of the Islamic Revolutionary Guards and close ally of Supreme Religious Leader Ayatollah Khamenei, are already apparent in the workings of the Ministry and, more generally, an atmosphere of renewed restriction to which numerous sources for this report attested. Two signs of this shift are the cancellation of invitations

---

[4] Some foundations in Iran, such as Bonyad-e Mostazafin (Foundation of the Dispossessed), led by Mohsen Rafiq-Doost, the former minister of the Islamic Revolutionary Guards, are explicitly recognized as government agencies. Others, such as Sazman Tabligath Islami (Islamic Propagation Organization), led by Hojatoleslam Ahmad Jannati -- also a member of the influential Council of Guardians -- and Bonyad-e Poonzdah Khordad (Fifteenth of Khordad Foundation), led by Hojatoleslam Hassan Sane'i, are nominally independent entities. Despite this distinction, most foundations are headed by influential clergy, and share the common goal of preserving and promoting the Islamic system and values. Also, they all find their origin in the aftermath to the 1979 revolution, when the new government bequeathed property it had confiscated to the private ownership of foundations, to be administered by their leadership. These foundations have since become independent and influential decision-making bodies, accountable to no government entity and sustained by their access to large amounts of capital. We refer to them collectively and for the sake of simplicity as semi-autonomous foundations.

[5] Chapter 2 assesses the political affiliation and state sponsorship of each of the eleven national dailies.

issued to the organizers of Western international film festivals to attend the Iranian Fajr Film Festival in February 1993, and increasingly frequent, unchecked vigilante attacks against the press and publishing houses in the past year. Another is the recent, severe crackdown on "vice and social corruption" in Tehran, which has included the arrests of more than 500 women in late June and ongoing arrests through July. The women were arrested for violations of the dress code such as wearing sunglasses; 300 men were also held for wearing short-sleeved T-shirts.[6]

MECHANISMS OF CONTROL

Limits on freedom of expression in Iran defy simple definition. It is not possible to trace censorship to any single source within the government structure. Rather, there often exists no regulation relevant to the "offense" at hand, and in a given case the Anti-Narcotics Section of the Islamic Revolutionary Prosecutor, the Ministry of Intelligence, a state-affiliated newspaper or a semi-autonomous foundation has as much de facto power to monitor expression as the government's designated official for this function, the Minister of Culture and Islamic Guidance.

In certain cases, censorship is accomplished by official banning orders, or through imprisonment and mistreatment of offenders. In most cases, the means of control are more subtle and indirect. The government exercises control "unofficially" through binding "suggestions" and "advice." Official orders are delivered orally and individuals directed to write them down in their own handwriting -- leaving no official paper trail. Other forms of government control include distribution of paper for books and newspapers, and setting prices for books and admission to films. The financial loss associated with books banned after publication and films banned after production also serves as an effective tool of government retribution.

To implement its censorship policies, the government relies on a variety of nongovernmental players. A common means of control and censorship are unchecked vigilante attacks against the press and publishing houses. In the 1992-1993 period alone, there have been at least nine such attacks in Tehran. At any time, any piece of work may become the object of attacks orchestrated primarily through the mass

---

[6] *New York Times*, June 23, 1993, p. A4, and *Iran Times*, July 2, 1993, p. 1.

media for being anti-Islamic and anti-revolutionary, regardless of whether the work has been previously approved by the government and issued a permit. Crowds of angry protestors or *hezbollahi*[7] may appear in the streets, vilifying the targeted individual, destroying and looting property, deriding "lax" government policies and demanding strict official retribution. These crowds often gather at the invitation of the state-affiliated media and generally act without meaningful police restraint or fear of prosecution.

Some officials may object to the *hezbollahis'* tactics, but blaming the victim is also common. In early June 1993, after sixty motorcyclists attacked a magazine, a spokesman for the Ministry of Culture and Islamic Guidance told the newspaper *Salam*, "We cannot stop them, but we also do not approve of their attitude and behavior." On the other hand, he said, "our publications should behave in a way not to offend the sentiments of the *hezbollahis*."[8]

Officials who take a stronger stance in defending expression are subject to attack themselves. For a system that lays claim to embodiment of Islamic principles, charges that one is anti-Islamic and anti-revolutionary carry great power. Especially in a government as divided within itself as that of the Islamic Republic of Iran, such charges serve as an effective way of putting state officials on the defensive. Once a politically-created *javv*[9] signals a sufficient level of instability and outrage within the ruling elite, the government responds by banning work, often previously approved, and imprisoning and prosecuting the individuals responsible. The accusation of who is *more* Islamic reverberates widely and strongly not only against the secular but the determinedly devout.

As anarchic as the process may appear, there is no evading censorship in Iran. Any person can become the indirect agent of

---

[7] *Hezbollahi* literally means "the partisans of God." They see themselves as followers of the path of Ayatollah Khomeini.

[8] Agence France-Presse, June 3, 1993, as reported in FBIS, June 4, 1993.

[9] In Persian, *javv* means atmosphere. This term has gained particular currency and significance in Iran since the revolution in reflection of the government's frequent and explicit reliance on the "public" mood and atmosphere in its policy making and application of the law. In order to better capture this phenomenon, the term *javv* will be used in this report.

censorship, be it the book publisher or the film producer who rejects or modifies work that may in any fashion be controversial out of fear of unbearable financial sanctions imposed by the government, and of prosecution. The artist or intellectual also is caught in the grip of self-censorship, remembering colleagues who in the past have lost their lives or liberty for their ideas, and facing everyday fear and uncertainty. The role of self-censorship in Iran cannot be underestimated. The hands of the government need descend on relatively few to silence many others.

SCOPE OF CONTROLS

Expression that poses a serious threat to the supremacy of the prevailing system -- by reaching large or crucial segments of society or by propagating alternate systems of thought and governance -- is not tolerated. On such matters, the government speaks with a single voice and decisively.

Freedom to organize political parties not aligned with the government and the freedom of such parties to express political views are strictly and uniformly prohibited, despite the constitutional guarantee of free association. Political speech that is genuinely independent or critical of the government is not tolerated. Offenders are sentenced before the Islamic Revolutionary Courts to long prison terms. There are also a large number of political executions in Iran.[10]

The Constitution places radio and television under the direct supervision of the religious leader and the three branches of government. Radio and television in Iran, a country that is forty-eight percent illiterate,[11] exclusively promote government policy, and the content of their programs is predominantly religious.

---

[10] It is extremely difficult to be precise about these cases. However, Amnesty International has estimated at least 2,500 political executions in 1988, the highest number for any year since the immediate post-revolutionary period. For 1991, AI documented 775 executions, of which at least sixty were the result of convictions on political charges; and for 1992, 330 executions of which at least 140 of the executed had been formally charged with political offenses.

[11] *The Europa World Yearbook 1992* (London: Europa Publications, 1992), Vol. I, p. 1422.

Educational control is also considered crucial to the government's consolidation of power. The faculty and curricula of all teaching institutions were purged and "Islamicized" during the revolution's first years, to ensure the ideological purity of the information available to young people. Universities, traditional centers of dissent under the monarchy, were closed for two years and, upon their reopening, were reserved for students ardently committed to the values of the revolution and the Islamic government. While ideological and character screening has abated in recent years, especially at the undergraduate level, it remains a persistent feature of the Iranian educational system for graduate and post-graduate studies. Since the reopening of the universities, approximately forty percent of student admittance has been reserved for released prisoners of war, the revolutionary guards, paramilitary volunteers (*bassiji*) and the relatives of martyrs. These students serve as the "eyes and ears" of the government authorities and report on those teachers and fellow students suspected of harboring anti-Islamic or anti-regime sentiments.

Denial and distortion of the Iran's pre-Islamic cultural heritage have also been strong components of the government's agenda. Celebration of the Iranian New Year, Nowruz, or the ancient Zoroastrian "fire festival" Chahar Shanbeh Soori was impeded by the authorities for years. This has also meant that literary giants whose work is not in line with the prevailing value system have been either banned outright, de-emphasized or reinterpreted. Significant public resistance has forced the government to abandon much of its original agenda, yet certain of its elements persist. Parents, for example, are denied a birth certificate if they plan to give their newborn child a name that connotes Iran's pre-Islamic or monarchical past.

The barriers of intolerance and control are compounded in the case of women. Women artists and intellectuals, and the depiction of women in art, are subject to severe constraints arising from tradition and superstition. While these impulses have strong social bases, the government has manipulated these traditions wherever possible to tighten controls and promote its preferred value system. Post-revolutionary law bars women from a number of fields in education and educated professions such as engineering, and severely restricts their personal freedoms. For example, after the 1934 mandatory unveiling imposed by Reza Shah, Iranian women must once again endure the excesses of the state, this time the mandatory veiling imposed since the revolution.

The scope of government control and censorship, as is well known, has extended across continents and oceans by way of a religious edict or *fatwa*. Ayatollah Khomeini's 1989 death sentence against novelist Salman Rushdie and all others associated with the publication of his book *The Satanic Verses* has already led to the murder of the novel's Japanese translator and the attempted murder of its Italian translator. Since the issuance of the *fatwa*, Rushdie himself has been forced to live in hiding. Iranians in exile who have supported Rushdie's right to expression, by openly condemning the death sentence against him, have been threatened with death as well, their work has been banned in Iran and their publishers threatened with reprisals.

Vigilante attacks and vilification campaigns in the state-affiliated press do not stop with criticism of the work deemed offensive or even character assassination of the artist or intellectual but extend as well to government officials, usually those within the Ministry of Culture and Islamic Guidance and even occasionally the President, and call into question their legitimacy to govern. In one instance reported here, employees of the Ministry were prosecuted alongside writers and publishers whose "anti-revolutionary" work they had approved.

The resignation of Mohammad Khatami, the Minister of Culture and Islamic Guidance, in July 1992 was brought about by such attacks. Khatami was an outspoken opponent of lawlessness and the influence of vigilante groups. His three-year term was a period of relative freedom for cultural and artistic endeavors, and in response to this, he was harshly criticized by hard-line newspapers such as *Keyhan* and by Supreme Religious Leader Ayatollah Khamenei. In his letter of resignation, submitted on May 24, 1992, he explained his departure by citing "the climate of insecurity that increasingly bedevils cultural activities" in Iran, warning that this situation threatened to condemn "intellectuals, artists and even faithful friends of the Islamic Revolution" to "indifference."[12]

---

[12] Agence France-Presse, July 18, 1992, as reported in FBIS, July 20, 1992. President Rafsanjani had refused to accept a previous resignation offer, but was eventually compelled to bow to the tide of hard-line opinion.

Background

Four periods of relative freedom of expression in Iranian modern history were the constitutional movement of 1905-1911; the years following the abdication from power of Reza Shah in favor of his son Mohammad Reza Shah, from 1941-1953; a period of political crisis from 1960-1963; and the revolutionary era from March 1978 to mid-1980. Each period ended as the ruling powers consolidated their power. Censorship and control are deeply rooted in Iran. Many who are censored, imprisoned and exiled today were similarly punished in the past.

In some respects, however, the current situation is unique. The nature of censorship in Iran cannot be separated from the system of governance established since the revolution of 1979 based on *velayat-i faqih* or the "guardianship of the jurisprudent."[13] *Velayat-i faqih* presupposes a need for supreme guidance in the average person's conduct of everyday affairs, and considers that the *faqih* is uniquely qualified to provide such guidance, dictating the single acceptable way of life or value system consistent with Shi'a Islam. Fundamental is the belief that every good and pious citizen, like a child, may be steered wrong by a "perverse" word, film or music, and thus what the citizen reads, sees and hears must be closely monitored by the governing authorities. Ayatollah Khomeini wrote in this regard:

> If someone should ask you, "Why has God, the All-Wise, appointed holders of authority and commanded you to obey them?" you should answer him as follows: . . . "[M]en would not be able to keep to their ordained path and to enact God's laws unless a trustworthy and protective individual (or power) were appointed over them with responsibility for this matter, to prevent them from stepping outside the sphere of the licit and transgressing against the rights of others."[14]

---

[13] A jurisprudent is one learned in the principles and ordinances of law; a *faqih* is a jurisprudent of Islamic law and faith.

[14] Khomeini, *Islam and Revolution*, p. 52.

Thus, censorship in Iran is not only proscriptive but also prescriptive. The Iranian writer, journalist, film director or painter is required to steer clear of sensitive topics, such as critical and candid assessment of the system of government, sources of authority and Islam. Additionally, however, he or she must write, direct or draw in a manner that conforms with the prevailing value system. In fact, the Constitution of the Islamic Republic of Iran and the Press Law of 1985 place on every Iranian citizen an affirmative duty to serve the prevailing Islamic value system and promote the "public good," as construed by the government.

The process of content control on the basis of Islamic principles, however, is complicated by the fact that Islam itself is subject to differing interpretations. In an interview with the magazine *Cinéaste*, film director Abbas Kiarostami stated:

> [I]n Iran, everyone has a completely different interpretation. They're free to think what they want. The danger comes when someone wants to say, "No, my interpretation is the only right one."[15]

The divergent interpretations of Islam are mirrored in the divisions within the governing elite -- especially as regards expression.

LEGAL FRAMEWORK

The laws governing public discourse in Iran provide no effective protection for dissent or even deviation. The Constitution's guarantee of freedom of expression is crippled by exceptions requiring compliance with "the fundamental principles of Islam or the rights of the public." The Press Law adds further debilitating exceptions. Provisions in both instruments, apart from setting the limits of discourse, also dictate its content: every citizen has the duty, in all aspects of his or her life, "to enjoin the good and forbid the evil," a Koranic phrase for the framework of the moral life. The press may not publish material that promotes "prostitution" or "wastefulness" or "harms the bases of the Islamic

---

[15] Miriam Rosen, "The Camera of Art: An Interview with Abbas Kiarostami," *Cinéaste*, Vol. XIX, Nos. 2-3, December 1992, p. 39.

Republic." Even eligibility to start a publication, under the Press Law, is limited to those who exhibit "moral fitness" for that function.

The Constitutional and Press Law provisions requiring that press offenses be tried openly and in the presence of a jury were ignored until 1992. In that year, the two separate trials of the editors of the magazines *Farad* and *Gardoon* were conducted in general courts and in the presence of the press jury. The press jury consists of clergy, government officials and editors of state-affiliated press. In one of these cases the initial stages of prosecution, prior to trial, were marked by violations of the Press Law and by the involvement of the Islamic Revolutionary Prosecutor.

Books, non-journalistic publications and films are regulated separately. Vaguely-worded requirements in the regulations on book publication make authors responsible for "guarding the positive outcomes of the Islamic revolution" and forbid them from writing anything that "profanes and denies the meanings of religion." A commission under the Ministry of Culture and Islamic Guidance oversees the publication of books and other printed matter. Filmmakers, on the other hand, are overseen by four councils within the Ministry -- one to review a summary of the screenplay, one to review the full screenplay, one to review the completed film and issue or withhold a release permit, and the fourth to review, occasionally, films denied a release permit. Forbidden topics in film include any that "denies or weakens the principles of Islam," "depicts foreign culture, politics, economy or society in a misleading manner," or "presents any material that is against the interests of the country."[16]

In the meantime, a number of offenses related to the press, writers and intellectuals based on the content of their work remained unlawfully before the Islamic Revolutionary Courts. Islamic Revolutionary Courts were instituted as a temporary measure to process the large numbers of people arrested in the aftermath of the 1979 revolution. They have since become a permanent feature of the Iranian legal system, and are notorious for their disregard of international standards of due process and for their harsh sentences. The government invokes the jurisdiction of the Revolutionary Courts in offenses which, in its opinion, are not punished severely enough by the general court -- disregarding the jurisdictional limits of these courts under domestic law. Thus, journalists and intellectuals may be prosecuted for the content of

---

[16] Regulations translated by Middle East Watch.

their work under the general rubric of acting "against internal or external security."

CASES

This report covers more than sixty incidents involving the prosecution, imprisonment or harassment of writers, filmmakers, journalists and intellectuals based on the content of their work. A few cases serve as illustrative.

The most widely known example of Iranian censorship is Ayatollah Khomeini's issuance of a religious edict or ***fatwa*** against a non-Iranian writer living outside Iran in response to the content of a novel. On February 14, 1989, Ayatollah Khomeini decreed that **Salman Rushdie**, author of *The Satanic Verses*, and all others associated with its publication were sentenced to death for apostasy and that it was a duty incumbent on every Muslim to enforce this sentence. The day after the edict, Hojatoleslam Hassan Sane'i, the head of the Fifteenth of Khordad Foundation, offered a bounty of $1 million to whomever carried out the death sentence; since then, the bounty has been twice increased, once in March 1991 to $2 million and again in February 1993 by an unspecified amount. Meanwhile, agents of the *fatwa* struck on different continents: in July 1991 both the novel's Japanese translator, Hitoshi Igarashi, and its Italian translator, Ettore Capriolo, were stabbed by unknown assailants -- the former fatally. Since 1989, Rushdie has lived in hiding and under police protection. Four years later, the *fatwa* remains in force and has been reiterated by leading Iranian government officials and by vote of its parliament.

Less well known are the reprisals against Iranians, living in exile, who have opposed the *fatwa*. On the third anniversary of the edict, a group of fifty Iranian writers, intellectuals and professionals in exile in Europe and the United States issued a declaration condemning the death sentence. In response, Ayatollah Janatti, a member of the Council of Guardians,[17] banned the works of all those signatories to the declaration.

---

[17] The Council of Guardians is an influential government entity, composed of six qualified Muslim jurists and six lay Muslim lawyers. It supervises elections and examines legislation adopted by the parliament, ensuring that it accords with the Constitution and with Islamic precepts.

The newspaper *Jumhouri-ye Islami,* affiliated with Supreme Religious Leader Ayatollah Khamenei, announced that those Iranians who spoke against the *fatwa* had joined the list of "infidels" deserving of the death sentence. Nevertheless, by the fourth anniversary of the edict, in February 1993, the number of signatories had increased to 162. The government has effectively banned the works of all the current signatories.

Two of Iran's best-known artists have been particularly outspoken critics of the Islamic Republic's censorship and harassment policies -- of which they themselves are targets. In the case of **Ali-Akbar Saidi-Sirjani,** a writer and social critic, the government initially notified him that it had no objection to his work. After eight of his books were published, however, the government banned their release, thereby imposing an unbearable financial burden on him, his family and his publishers. All his other work is now also banned.

Film director **Bahram Beizai** has also suffered under government-imposed financial constraints and self-censorship. In response to influential pressure groups, the government required extensive modification of his most recent film, *Mosaferan* (Travelers) -- after having previously censored, issued an approval permit and even given an award to the film. He was denied the right to travel with another of his films to an international film festival in 1992, the screening of which was approved by the Iranian government. For thirteen years, he has been unable to work in the theater due to the withdrawal of his work permit.

Prison, fifty lashes and the prospect of further imprisonment are the price that cartoonist **Manouchehr Karimzadeh** has paid since the April 1992 banning of the science magazine *Farad,* which carried a drawing of an apparently crippled soccer player who, for some readers, resembled the late Ayatollah Khomeini. Tried not in general court as required for press offenses but in the Islamic Revolutionary Court, as if he had attacked national security, Karimzadeh was sentenced to one year in prison for having created that drawing. In blatant disregard for his rights, almost at the end of his prison term, the Supreme Court "revoked" his sentence and required that he be "re-tried." A trial date has yet to be announced.

Women artists and intellectuals, and the depiction of women in art, are subject to especially strict constraints, and any deviation from government norms is treated with severity. **Shahrnoush Parsipour,** a novelist of much acclaim, was twice imprisoned by the Islamic

Revolutionary Prosecutor for her book *Zanan Bedoun-e Mardan* (Women Without Men), once with her publisher **Mohammad-Reza Aslani**. They were tried in the general courts along with two officials of the Ministry of Culture and Islamic Guidance who had reviewed and issued a permit for her book, and all four were acquitted. Despite their acquittal, Aslani's publishing house, Nashr-e Nogreh, was bombed by vigilantes, and Parsipoor's work remains banned.

Another woman novelist, **Moniroo Ravanipoor**, who draws her inspiration from Iranian folk tales, started experiencing censorship with the banning of her book *Sanghay Sheytan* (Devil's Stones) after vehement attacks in the press in 1990. After this banning, her previously published work was subject to more intensive scrutiny and censorship at subsequent printings. Her book *Kanizoo* was banned in 1991 at its third printing; it was published in 1993 after twenty months of negotiated modifications.

Historical, literary and cultural texts not in line with the prevailing ideology are revised, reinterpreted or banned outright. The life-long work of **Ahmad Shamlu**, a renowned modern poet, has been banned on this basis. His *Ketab-e Koucheh* (Book of the Street) is a compilation of 120 volumes of popular Persian sayings, slang and proverbs. The popular lexicon in Iran has strong secular and anti-clerical elements.

Mohsen Makhmalbaf entered the film industry after the revolution with a history of imprisonment under the Shah and strong *hezbollahi* convictions. But, when his fourth and fifth films examined the poverty and hopelessness of daily life for some Iranians, official attitudes hardened: two of his later films were banned and a third censored. Most recently, Makmalbaf sought the film board's approval for a script on the 1991 Gulf war, and it was rejected partly on the grounds that it had not sufficiently focused on the plight of the Shi'a people. (Iran's population is overwhelmingly Shi'a, as is its ruling clergy.)

The government, acutely aware of the influence of the foreign news media, generally treats foreign journalists well once they are allowed to enter the country. Iranian journalists working for foreign news organizations, however, are particularly vulnerable to government pressure and manipulation. With the permission of the government, Iranian photojournalist **Kaveh Golestan** prepared a video on the situation of journalists working in Iran, which presented an unvarnished portrait of the constraints on expression. He lost his journalist card in June 1992 after the video was broadcast in England and its transcript published by the free-expression group Index on Censorship. He has also been prevented from leaving Iran. The government has not indicated the basis for its ongoing "investigation" of Golestan and the cancellation of his accreditation.

Jahangir Jahanbagloo, an Iranian journalist, had his journalist card canceled by the Ministry of Culture and Islamic Guidance in November 1992. He has been the official representative of the American television network NBC in Iran since 1991. Over the past nine months, the Ministry has failed to provide any meaningful explanation for its cancellation of his accreditation. The financial consequences to Jahanbagloo have been serious.

Upon his return to Iran to cover a news report for a foreign television network, an Iranian freelance cameraman, **Bahram Molaie**, was arrested in 1987. Without being charged or tried for any offense, he was imprisoned for forty-five days, and his accreditation was canceled. Long after his release from prison, in 1991, the government informed him that there was nothing in his file, and that it was now closed. He is still unable to work as a journalist in Iran, however.

The Press Law, passed in 1985, was applied for the first time in 1992 for the prosecution of two magazines editors before the general courts and with a press jury. However, the Islamic Revolutionary Prosecutor was unlawfully involved in the preliminary stages of one case. In both instances, government prosecutions were initiated as a follow-up to mob attacks against the offices of the magazines.

Nasser Arabha, editor of the science magazine *Farad*, was imprisoned pending trial, then tried and sentenced to six months imprisonment on the charge of "acting against internal security." *Farad* had published a cartoon deemed by the government to be insulting to Ayatollah Khomeini. The magazine remains banned.

The Islamic Revolutionary Prosecutor, exceeding his mandate and usurping the functions of the general courts, indicted **Abbas Maroufi**, editor of the cultural magazine *Gardoon*, for insulting and spreading rumors against the holy system and propagating monarchical culture, and banned the magazine. The cover of the August 1992 issue of *Gardoon* was deemed anti-revolutionary. Although finally acquitted in criminal court, Maroufi was not able to resume publication of the magazine immediately after trial. A government representative "unofficially" informed him that he should not publish his magazine until the *javv* was more appropriate, and that the government could not be responsible for his life if he defied the suggestion. The magazine subsequently resumed publication.

Recently, one magazine was banned and another attacked by unchecked vigilantes on political grounds.

In April 1993, the magazine *Rah-e Mojahed* published by **Lotfollah Meissami** was banned for printing statements by Ayatollah Hossein Ali Montazeri. At one time the designated successor to Ayatollah Khomeini, Montazeri is now an opponent and critic of Supreme Religious Leader Ayatollah Khamenei and President Rafsanjani.

In May 1993, the office of the scientific magazine *Kiyan* was attacked by a group of motorcycle riders who called for the closure of the magazine and the death of its editor, **Reza Tehrani**. At issue was an interview the magazine had published with Mehdi Bazargan, the former Prime Minister and head of the banned political organization Nehzat-Azadi (Freedom Movement).

RECOMMENDATIONS

To the extent that the atmosphere for expression in Iran has improved since the early years of the revolution, a large measure of credit must go to the Iranians who have been determined to continue speaking, writing, creating and thinking as they choose. Yet recent indications are that even this small opening may be closing up again. The Iranian government must change its policies to protect their right of free expression, both through legal provisions that guarantee protection and through the punishment of acts that seek to undermine that protection.

(1) To the government of Iran

Middle East Watch calls upon the Iranian government to amend its laws so as to comply with international legal standards on freedom of expression:

•Amend the Constitution to remove those portions that restrict the exercise of free expression (e.g. Arts. 9 and 24), such that speech is protected consistent with international instruments to which Iran is a party;

•Replace the existing Press Law with legislation whose definition of libel and registration requirements for publications do not infringe on protected speech and freedom of opinion.

Furthermore, in order to bring state conduct into conformity with international law, Middle East Watch calls on the government of Iran to:

•Abolish book and film censorship boards;

•Cease all legal actions against newspaper editors, journalists, writers, publishers and political activists that are based on criticism or deviation from government policy;

•Bring about the rescission of Ayatollah Khomeini's *fatwa* against Salman Rushdie and others associated with the publication of *The Satanic Verses*, and the cancellation of the bounty offered by the Fifteenth of Khordad Foundation for the murder of the author.

•Bring about the rescission of the *fatwa* as extended to the 162 Iranian signatories to the declaration condemning the death sentence against Rushdie; and annul official restrictions on the presentation and publication of their works in Iran;

•Prosecute vigilante groups that attack and destroy property and threaten lives in cases involving the press, book publishers and other targets chosen in reprisal for their views;

•End the use of government-distributed paper (e.g. for books and the press) and government-set prices (e.g. for books and film) as means of control and censorship;

•Issue all government orders and directives officially and in writing;

•Abolish ideologically-based criteria for admission to university.

In order to encourage free and diverse expression, Middle East Watch calls on the government to:

•Allow non-governmental voices access to state-owned radio and television;

•Permit the establishment of independent radio and television stations;

•Permit the establishment and circulation of privately-owned and -published newspapers and political magazines.

Finally, Middle East Watch urges Iran to reverse its recent policy of denying entry to the U.N. Special Representative, Mr. Galindo-Pohl.

2) To the European Community

Middle East Watch calls upon the European Community to:

•Adopt a Community-wide position that decisions regarding any EC aid and aid from individual member states to the Iranian government -- other than that for humanitarian purposes -- will be linked to grave abuses of the right to free expression, including the *fatwa* against Salman Rushdie and those associated with *The Satanic Verses* and the bounty for Rushdie's murder, and the Iranian government's arbitrary detentions and prosecutions of journalists, writers, filmmakers and artists on the basis of their opinions, as well as violent intimidation of such persons by groups that operate with impunity;

•Pass a strong resolution highlighting the overlooked plight of those Iranian artists and intellectuals whose right to free expression inside Iran is seriously curtailed, and of the 162 exiled Iranian writers and artists who have publicly condemned the *fatwa*. The Council of Ministers should warn Iran that any attack on Iranian dissident writers, artists and intellectuals living in EC member countries will be treated as an attack on any EC citizen; and

•Use the leverage provided by its growing trade and investment links with Iran, to press Iranian officials to permit a broad range of political and artistic expression.

(3) To other trading partners of Iran

Middle East Watch urges these nations, in particular Japan, to:

- Use the leverage provided by their trade and investment contacts with Iran, to press Iranian officials to permit a broad range of political and artistic expression; and

- Warn Iran that any attack on Iranian dissident writers, artists and intellectuals living in their national territories will be treated as an attack on a citizen of their countries.

(4) To the United States

Middle East Watch urges the U.S. government to add to its already strong position on Iran the public declaration that any attack on Iranian dissident writers, artists and intellectuals living in the United States will be treated as an attack on a U.S. citizen.

1
LEGAL FRAMEWORK

INTERNATIONAL LAW

As a member of the international community of nations and as a signatory to the International Covenant on Civil and Political Rights,[1] Iran is bound by universal norms guaranteeing freedom of expression. The Iranian government of President Ali Akbar Hashemi-Rafsanjani is in violation of these norms.

Article 19 of the Covenant reads in part:

> (1) Everyone shall have the right to hold opinions without interference.
>
> (2) Everyone shall have the right to freedom of expression; this right shall include freedom to seek, receive and impart information and ideas of all kinds, regardless of frontiers, either orally, in writing or in print, in the form of art, or through any other media of his choice.

Violations of Article 19 must be punished by the government "notwithstanding that the violation has been committed by persons acting in an official capacity (Article 2(3)(a))." The government is required to ensure that any person whose rights or freedoms are violated shall have an effective remedy, which includes adopting "such legislative or other measures as may be necessary to give effect to the rights recognized" in the Covenant (Art. 2(2)). It also provides that a "competent judicial, administrative or legislative" authority determine the rights of a person claiming such remedy; and that a "competent" authority enforce such remedies when granted (Art. 2(3)).

Furthermore, Article 17 protects individuals against unlawful attacks on their dignity and property by anyone and imposes on the government a duty to safeguard this right. Article 17 reads:

---

[1] The International Covenant on Civil and Political Rights was signed by Iran on April 4, 1968, and ratified on June 24, 1975.

> 1. No one shall be subjected to arbitrary or unlawful interference with his privacy, family, home or correspondence, nor to unlawful attacks on his honour and reputation.
>
> 2. Everyone has the right to the protection of the law against such interference or attacks.

Article 20 is also relevant to this report, specifically with reference to the *fatwa* against Salman Rushdie and all others associated with *The Satanic Verses*. Article 20 states that "Any advocacy of national, racial or religious hatred that constitutes incitement to discrimination, hostility or violence shall be prohibited by law."[2]

Finally, the Covenant is drafted in accordance with the Universal Declaration of Human Rights, in recognition of the fact that freedom from fear is inherent to the ideal of free human beings, and that such freedom is achieved only when an individual can enjoy his or her rights without fear of arbitrary and unlawful government interference. The Preamble reads in part:

> [T]he ideal of free human beings enjoying civil and political freedom and freedom from fear and want can only be achieved if conditions are created whereby everyone may enjoy his civil and political rights, as well as his economic, social and cultural rights . . . .

[2] Human Rights Watch policy on "hate speech," as relevant to the *fatwa*, is noted in Chapter 7. Our interpretation of Article 20 heavily favors protecting freedom of speech, including speech that focuses hostility on a group; but the *fatwa* is exceptionally specific and therefore violates Article 20.

DOMESTIC LAW

Constitution of the Islamic Republic of Iran [3]

The Iranian Constitution's guarantees of freedom of expression are subject to qualifications that effectively impede the free exchange of information and ideas. Freedom of expression is conditional on compliance with the government's interpretation of Islamic norms and public interest. Article 24 reads:

> Publications and the press have freedom of expression except when it is detrimental to the fundamental principles of Islam or the rights of the public. The details of this exception will be specified by law.

Furthermore, the "political, cultural, economic, and military independence or the territorial integrity of Iran" may not be infringed in any manner "under the pretext of exercising freedoms" (Art. 9). These provisions of the Constitution have been applied by the government to restrict speech.

Other provisions of the Constitution intended to protect speech have been largely ignored, such as Article 168, which states that "political and press offenses will be tried openly and in the presence of a jury, in courts of justice." Similarly ignored have been Article 23, which prohibits prosecution of any person "simply for holding a certain belief," and Article 25, which prohibits censorship unless provided by law.

In the final analysis, the Constitution permits control of expression by requiring that every citizen's conduct, including speech, serve the government's notion of propriety. Article 8 imposes on every citizen of the Islamic Republic of Iran an affirmative and perpetual duty "to enjoin the good and forbid the evil," pursuant to the identical Koranic injunction.

In January 1992, the Head of the Judiciary Ayatollah Mohammad Yazdi announced, "Courts of justice and judiciary branches have been notified that all press and political trials must be held in the presence of juries and attorneys." Otherwise, he added, "the verdicts will be nullified

---

[3] This report cites the Constitution of the Islamic Republic of Iran as amended in 1989 and translated by the state-affiliated Islamic Propagation Organization.

by the Supreme Court."[4] Yet prosecution of some press and political offenses were subsequently initiated and/or tried by the Islamic Revolutionary Court. Notable examples are the prosecution of cartoonist Manouchehr Karimzadeh and the indictment and imprisonment of novelist Shahrhoush Parsipour and her publisher, Reza Aslani (see Chapters 2 and 6).

Press Law[5]

The Press Law was ratified in 1985. It applies only to publications that appear regularly with sequenced numbers (Art. 1). Novels and other books do not come under the authority of this law.

Article 2 of the Press Law expands on the constitutional and religious duty to "enjoin the good and forbid the evil" and contemplates a specific role and content for the press, which consist of the following:

> (A) To enlighten public opinion and to raise the level of people's knowledge and awareness in one or more of the areas listed in Article 1 (e.g. news, commentary, social, political, economic, agricultural, religious, scientific, technical, military, art and sports).
>
> (B) To promote the goals that are expressed in the Constitution.
>
> (C) To struggle against false and divisive classifications and to avoid pitting different strata in society against one another on the basis of race, language, tradition and custom . . . [sic]
>
> (D) To fight against the manifestations of colonial culture (e.g. prodigality, waste, vanity, luxury and spread

---

[4] *Iran Focus* (U.K.), Vol. 5, No. 1, Jan-Feb. 1992, cited in Article 19, *Iran: Press Freedom Under the "Moderates"* (London: 1992), p. 10.

[5] Since there exists no official translation of the Press Law, the provisions cited in this report have been translated by Middle East Watch.

of prostitution) and to promote and propagate authentic Islamic culture and diffuse virtuous principles.

(E) To protect and strengthen the policy of "neither East, nor West."[6]

In addition to this affirmative duty to educate and promote particular values and ideologies, the press is prohibited from engaging in discourse "harmful" to the principles and mandate of Islam and public rights. Article 6 sets broadly defined restraints for the press, which forbid publishing material that promotes "prostitution" or "wastefulness;" "creates divisions among the different strata of society," in particular on the grounds of racial or tribal affiliation; "harms the bases of the Islamic Republic;" or threatens the "security, integrity and interests of the" state. These prohibitions are subject to much manipulation and arbitrary use by government officials.

Contradicting all the restraints noted above, Article 4 of the Press Law categorically forbids all censorship and control of the press. It reads: "No official or unofficial authority has the right to exert pressure on the press for the publication of any material or article, or attempt to censor or control the press." However, the terms of this provision have not been honored.

The Press Law requires that press offenses be prosecuted before a jury in the courts of general jurisdiction (Art. 34). Every two years, a council composed of the head of the judiciary, head of the city council or alternatively the mayor, and a representative from the Ministry of Culture and Islamic Guidance meets to select the press jury.[7] The council selects fourteen people "who are trusted by the public" from a variety of social groups including: "clergy, university professors, medical doctors, writers, journalists, lawyers, teachers, heads of notary offices,

---

[6] This slogan gained currency during the revolution. It represents the government's stated intent to be completely independent from Western as well as Eastern countries, especially in political and cultural spheres.

[7] Article 31 of the 1979 Press Law governs the composition and terms of the press jury. The 1985 Press Law is silent on these matters. The relevant provisions have been translated by Middle East Watch.

guilds, tradesmen, workers and farmers." Seven serve as the original jury, while seven are on reserve. Members of the press jury must meet three prerequisites. They must: be at least thirty years of age, have no criminal record, and be "known for trustworthiness and sincerity and have a good reputation."

After completion of deliberations and closure of case, the press jury must decide two questions: (a) Is the accused guilty? and (b) In the case of a finding of guilt, does the criminal deserve a reduced sentence?

The vote of the majority of the jury members is submitted in writing to the court. The court reaches a decision based on the jury's findings. If the jury has found the accused guilty, application of the law and determination of the punishment are the sole prerogative of the court.

Press matters are monitored by a five-member council in the Ministry of Culture and Islamic Guidance (Art. 36).[8] The council, either on its own initiative or that of the Ministry, looks into allegations of press offenses (Art. 12), and if legal action is deemed necessary, the council is required to submit a written statement requesting prosecution to the "court of competent jurisdiction" (Art. 12).

Despite these provisions, in practice other government agencies, notably the Islamic Revolutionary Prosecutor, have maintained control over the monitoring and prosecution of press offenses.

The Islamic Revolutionary Courts

At the instigation of Ayatollah Khomeini, the Revolutionary Council[9] established the Islamic Revolutionary Courts on June 17, 1979, as a temporary measure to process the large numbers of people arrested in the aftermath of the revolution. The Courts have settled into permanence, however. Their jurisdiction, as amended in 1983, encompasses:

---

[8] The council consists of a judge from the Supreme Court, a high-ranking official of the Ministry of Culture and Islamic Guidance, a representative from the Majlis or parliament, a university professor and a representative of the guild of newspaper editors (Art. 10).

[9] The legislative functions of the Islamic Republic were performed by this body prior to the election of the first Islamic Consultative Assembly.

> Any offence against internal or external security, attempt on the life of political personalities, any offence relating to narcotic drugs and smuggling, murder, massacre, imprisonment and torture in an attempt to fortify the Pahlavi regime,[10] suppressing the struggles of the Iranian people by giving orders or acting as agent, plundering the public treasury, profiteering and forestalling the market of public commodities.[11]

The government invokes the jurisdiction of the Revolutionary Courts in offenses, including those relating to journalists, writers and intellectuals, which in its opinion are not punished severely enough by the general courts. The Islamic Revolutionary Courts have been widely criticized for their disregard for due process and harsh sentences. Trials in the Islamic Revolutionary Courts are routinely held behind closed doors, without assistance of counsel or the right to present witnesses, and without the right to appeal.[12]

Regulations Governing Book Publication

Book publication is governed by regulations issued by the Ministry of Culture and Islamic Guidance which were ratified in 1988.[13] Books and publications must serve a particular objective in the Islamic

---

[10] The Pahlavis were the last Iranian royal dynasty. The wording of this clause reveals the insecurity of the Islamic regime four years after the revolution.

[11] Lawyers Committee for Human Rights, *The Justice System of the Islamic Republic of Iran* (New York: May 1993), p. 31.

[12] Among those who have documented and criticized such abuses are Amnesty International and the Special Representative of the U.N. Commission on Human Rights, Mr. Raynaldo Galindo-Pohl. Thousands of prisoners have been sentenced to death, imprisonment and other penalties by the Revolutionary Courts since 1979. See, for example, Lawyers Committee for Human Rights, *The Justice System*, pp. 30-36.

[13] Translation by Middle East Watch.

Republic. Article 3(A)(5) of the regulations outlines these objectives, which include "encouraging" the following:

(a) Strengthening and expanding research, as a principle means of gaining cultural independence and increasing the public's knowledge and ability to choose.

(b) Reasonable and knowledgeable defense of political, economic, and cultural independence, especially in favor of the principle "neither East, nor West."

(c) Guarding the positive outcomes of the Islamic revolution, and struggling to strengthen and expand these outcomes.

(d) Introducing the Islamic revolution through the compilation and publication of valuable scientific and cultural works.

Article 3(B) of the regulations indicates which books or publications are damaging to the principles of Islam and the right of the public and thus are not worthy of publication. It prohibits all material which:

(1) ...[P]rofanes and denies the meanings of religion.

(2) Propagates prostitution and moral corruption.

(3) Incites the public to an uprising against and opposition to the order of the Islamic Republic of Iran.

(4) Propagates the objectives of destructive and unlawful groups and strayed sects, and defends monarchic and dictatorial regimes.

(5) Creates unrest and conflict between tribes and religious groups, and injures the unity of society and the territorial integrity of the country.

(6) Insults or weakens national pride and patriotism, and creates loss of self-confidence before the culture, civilization and imperialistic regimes of the West or East.

(7) Propagates dependence on a global power and objects to the line of thinking based on preserving the independence of the country.

Article 4 of the regulations requires that the Ministry set up a commission to oversee compliance of book publications with Article 24 of the Constitution. The Ministry must select at least five persons for the commission. These persons must be "knowledgeable persons or persons in the science or culture fields familiar with issues pertaining to books, publication and social, political and propaganda affairs."

Chapter 6 describes in detail the censorship process for the publication of books.

Regulations Governing Film Production

Film production is governed by regulations issued by the Ministry of Culture and Islamic Guidance, which were ratified in 1989.[14]

Four councils within the Ministry are involved in the supervision, production and censorship of film:

Shoray-e Baresi Filmnameh (Council of Screenplay Inspection) -- This council reviews a summary of the screenplay for approval. It is composed of five persons selected by the Ministry's Bureau for Supervision and Evaluation (Edareh Koh-e Nezarat va Arzeshyabi) and the undersecretary of the Ministry's film division, and approved by the Minister of Culture and Islamic Guidance. These persons must be knowledgeable in cultural and artistic affairs and have expertise in the writing of screenplays.

Shoray-e Sodoor Parvaneh Filmsazi (Council for Issuing a Production Permit) -- This council inspects the full text of the screenplay and determines whether it can be produced. It is composed of five persons knowledgeable in matters pertaining to film and cinema, selected by the Bureau for Supervision and Evaluation and the undersecretary of the Ministry's film division, and approved by the Minister of Culture and Islamic Guidance. They include: a "filmmaking expert"; "production and management expert"; an expert familiar with cultural and artistic affairs"; and a representative from the Bureau for Supervision and Evaluation.

---

[14] Translated by Middle East Watch.

Shoray-e Bazbini (Council of Film Reviewing) -- This council reviews the completed film and determines whether it should be issued a release permit. It consists of the following five persons: "a cleric familiar with artistic matters"; "three persons with political, social and Islamic awareness and familiarity with film and cinema"; and "an expert in film matters and domestic and foreign cinema." A person from the Bureau for Supervision and Evaluation is present in the council's deliberations and is given the right to vote only when he or she serves as a substitute for an absent member of the council.

Shoray-e Ali-e Nezarat (High Council of Deputies) -- This council in certain circumstances reviews films which have not been issued a permit by the Council of Film Reviewing. It consists of a senior representative of the Ministry of Culture and Islamic Guidance; the undersecretary of the Ministry's film division; the undersecretary of the Ministry's cultural division; the undersecretary of the Ministry's artistic division; and a senior official from the Bureau for Supervision and Evaluation.

In March 1993, the government publicly released regulations governing film content that we excerpt below. (A more limited roster of content restrictions had been made public in recent years and the Ministry's technical regulations -- governing the steps to be taken for film approval -- have been in force for a decade.) These regulations[15] prohibit all material which:

• Denies or weakens the principles of Islam.

• Subverts Islam by propagating superstition and sorcery.

• Insults directly or indirectly God's messengers, *vali-ye faqih,* the Leadership Council or qualified *mojtaheds* [those learned in Islamic law].

• Profanes the sanctities of Islam and of other religions recognized in the Constitution of the Islamic Republic of Iran.

---

[15] *Siyasat-ha va Ravesh-ha-ye Ejraye Toleed, Tozih va Namayesh Filmhayeh Sinama-e 1372* (Politics and Methods of Film Production, Distribution and Screening 1993, an official publication) as reproduced in *Film,* March/April 1993, p. 41. Translation by Middle East Watch.

•Denies humankind's equality on the basis of color, race, language or ethnicity, negates the supremacy of virtue over all other considerations, and aggravates racial and ethnic differences.

•Denies or weakens the highest qualities of humankind (the veil, the spirit of forgiveness, sacrifice, modesty and . . .). [sic]

•Depicts or mentions situations that are against Islamic virtue (slander, use of tobacco products . . .). [sic]

•Propagates vile acts, corruption, prostitution and improper wearing of the veil.

•Educates on the topic of or encourages dangerous and injurious addictions and illicit professions such as smuggling.

•Depicts foreign culture, politics, economy or society in a misleading manner.

•States or presents any material that is against the interests of the country and can be exploited by foreigners.

•Depicts scenes of murder, torture and inhumane treatment in a manner that could cause viewers grief or miseducate them.

•Expresses or depicts historic and geographic facts, and the internal problems of the country in an exaggerated way or in a manner that misleads the viewer and offends the principles of Islam.

•Depicts unpleasant sounds or scenes (including those caused by technical defects) that could jeopardize the viewer's health.

•Involves films with low artistic or technical value that could lead to a decline in the public's taste and sensibilities.

Even after securing the necessary permits for production and release of a film, the regulations allow the undersecretary of the Ministry's film division to postpone the screening of a film in response to the necessities of political and cultural circumstances.

Chapter 8 describes in detail the role of the councils and the censorship process for the production of film.

2
THE PRESS

The number of publications in Iran has fluctuated significantly since the revolution. At the present time, it has once again risen to relatively high levels: in early 1993, the France-based organization Reporters Sans Frontières estimated that there were 560 publications nationwide, including thirty-three dailies, 105 weeklies, 221 monthly and twenty-five bi-monthly publications. But these bare numbers misrepresent the narrow range of tolerated discourse and the strict mechanisms of control. The current state of the press also provides a stark contrast to the wide diversity of opinion that was expressed in publications during the revolutionary period.

By the middle of 1979, it is estimated that more than 260 government- or privately-owned papers were being published in Iran, almost twice the number published prior to the revolution.[1] In the period known as the "Spring of Freedom," from March 1978 to mid-1980, many previously banned or underground publications were sold and distributed openly. Public debate and criticism centered on the possible and emerging forms of governance. Soon after consolidating its power, however, the ruling elite that emerged from the revolutionary struggles set about restricting newly-gained freedoms. As part of a progressive tightening of control, in a famous speech in November 1980 Ayatollah Khomeini asked the government: "Why do you not stop these newspapers? Why do you not shut their mouths? Why do you not stop their pens?"[2]

The governmental onslaught against the press started within months of the February 1979 revolution, as religious groups loyal to Ayatollah Khomeini took over the major Tehran daily newspapers *Keyhan* and *Ettela'at*. It intensified in August 1979 with the Revolutionary Council's passage of a new press law, which was intended to bring the media under government control. The 1979 Press Law required that all existing publications obtain a license within three months; many publications closed as a result. This onslaught culminated in June 1981 with a state of siege against all political opposition organizations and the

---

[1] *Ayandeh* (Iran), Vol. 5, Nos. 10-12, Winter 1979, pp. 916-921.

[2] Shaul Bakhash, *The Reign of the Ayatollahs; Iran and the Islamic Revolution* (New York: Basic Books, 1984), p. 148.

closure of their publications. During this period, the owners and staff of newspapers, publishing houses and bookstores were targets of imprisonment, and executions were common. For a time, the press struggled to survive and maintain its independence in the face of increasing restrictions and mob attacks, but to no avail.

A more comprehensive press law was approved by the Majlis after lengthy deliberations in January 1985, setting out operating guidelines for newspapers and magazines. Unlike books and films, which must be issued a permit prior to their release, newspapers and magazines are controlled primarily through mechanisms that are triggered once they have been published. Article 21 of the Press Law requires that two copies of every issue published be submitted automatically to the Ministry of Culture and Islamic Guidance. Printed opinion or reportage that exceeds the narrow limits of acceptable discourse may lead to retaliation including unchecked mob attacks, the suspension or closure of publishing facilities, and the prosecution and imprisonment of those responsible. Integral to the government's control of the press is the self-censorship bred by writers' and editors' fear of such retribution.

The government's failure or refusal to renew permits also serves as a retributive mechanism. Article 8 of the Press Law requires that print media obtain a permit from the Ministry before commencing publication. Article 7(A) prohibits the printing of publications which do not have permits, or those whose permits have been invalidated or cancelled temporarily or permanently, by court order. The Ministry's five-member press council[3] is required to specify the reasons for its rejection of a publication request, notifying the Ministry of Culture and Islamic Guidance of its decision within three months (Arts. 11 and 13). Two months after the acceptance of a request, the Ministry must issue a publication permit, and the publication must appear within the following six months (Arts. 13 and 16).

The Press Law severely restricts eligibility to start a publication. The right to publish newspapers and magazines is limited to those Iranian citizens who exhibit what the government considers to be moral fitness (Art. 9(4)). Those who held official positions between 1963 and 1978, those associated with the Shah's regime, and those who supported that regime are explicitly precluded from publishing newspapers or

---

[3] See Chapter 1 for discussion of the press council.

magazines (Art. 9). Iranian journalists also are required to obtain accreditation from the Ministry of Culture and Islamic Guidance.

The following section assesses the political affiliation of national newspapers. It then describes instances of government prosecution of newspaper and magazine staff, and of unchecked mob violence against the press. The section concludes with the case of Manouchehr Karimzadeh, prosecuted for a cartoon appearing in *Farad* magazine.

STATE-AFFILIATED NEWSPAPERS

Political Affiliation of National Newspapers

All newspapers derive their funding from and serve as mouthpieces for the government, semi-autonomous foundations or influential clergy. There exist no truly independent newspapers in Iran.[4] Newspapers nevertheless reflect widely divergent views on governance and policy, within the restricted paradigm of an Islamic government. Their pages often serve as the prime battleground for ideological debate, factional conflict and character assassination. An editorial in the pro-Rafsanjani *Tehran Times* of July 1992 stated:

> Most newspapers were afflicted with self-censorship or with a kind of party and group vengeance because, after the victory of the revolution, officials in charge of the country's important newspapers were mainly comprised of two parts: those who desired to use the newspapers as a ladder of success to reach higher state posts or those who left posts as ministers and top officials and fell in

[4] This phenomenon is widely and publicly acknowledged in Iran. For example, Hojatoleslam Ali Akbar Mohtashemi, a prominent member of the Tehran Combatant Clergy Association (breakaway group) -- a coalition of opponents of the Rafsanjani government (see footnote 7) -- stated in an interview with the newspaper *Salam*:"[I]f a newspaper is affiliated with a government organization, the proprietor of the said newspaper or magazine can only do what the said organization dictates that it do." *Salam*, May 16, 1993, as reported in FBIS, May 28, 1993.

status and turned to the press to be present in the country's politico-economic scene.[5]

There are twelve national daily newspapers currently published in Iran, including two in English. A listing of daily newspapers follows with a profile of each one's affiliation; the first two newspapers, *Keyhan* and *Ettela'at*, are government-owned. The remaining newspapers are state-affiliated:

•*Keyhan*[6] (Galaxy) -- This paper is the continuation of one of the best known pre-revolutionary dailies after its property was expropriated by the state-owned Bonyad-e Mostazafin (Foundation of the Dispossessed) and its staff purged in 1979. Its subsidiary, *Keyhan-e Hava'i,* is published and distributed abroad in Persian with several pages in English. It is aligned with the *hezbollahi* faction, and its editor-in-chief is directly appointed by the Supreme Religious Leader.

•*Ettela'at* (Information) -- This paper is also the continuation of one of the most known pre-revolutionary daily, after its property was expropriated by the state-owned Bonyad-e Mostazafin (Foundation of the Dispossessed) and its staff purged in 1979. It follows a conservative pro-clergy line often sympathetic to President Rafsanjani and with considerable following inside the Majlis. Its editor-in-chief is directly appointed by the Supreme Religious Leader.

•*Keyhan International* (English-language) -- This is the daily English subsidiary of *Keyhan* published in Iran.

•*Jomhouri-ye Islami* (Islamic Republic) -- It was instituted by the now defunct Islamic Republic Party in 1979, and, is presently associated with

---

[5] July 27, 1992; as cited in *Report on the Situation of Human Rights in the Islamic Republic of Iran by the Special Representative of the Commission on Human Rights*, Mr. Reynaldo Galindo-Pohl, (U.N. Doc. E/CN.4/1993/41), Jan. 28, 1993 [hereinafter U.N. Jan. 1993], at para. 179.

[6] *Keyhan* should not be mistaken with London *Keyhan* cited elsewhere in this report. London *Keyhan* is published in London by the previous owners of *Keyhan* in Iran before it was confiscated after the revolution.

Supreme Religious Leader Ayatollah Ali Khamenei. It is firmly in favor of a theocratic state dominated by clergymen and against Western ties.

•*Salam* (Hello) -- This paper started publishing in October 1990 and is associated with the group of clergy who broke off from the governing elite and formed the Majma'-e Rowhaniyun-e Mobarez-e Tehran (Tehran Combatant Clergy Association) (the breakaway group).[7] The manager and licensed publisher of the paper is Hojatoleslam Mohammad Musavi-Kho'iniha. It strictly follows the line of the late Ayatollah Khomeini and is critical of the economic, cultural and foreign policies of President Rafsanjani.

•*Jahan-e Islam* (World of Islam) -- This paper was instituted in 1991 and is headed by Hadi Khamenei, the brother of Supreme Religious Leader Ayatollah Khamenei. It also strictly follows the line of the late Ayatollah Khomeini and is critical of the President's policies. It is similar to *Salam* in political ideology.

•*Kar-va-Kargar* (Work and the Worker) -- This paper is published by Khaney-e Kargar (House of Workers), a workers' syndicate with strong religious and state affiliations, that voices workers' grievances with employers. Hossein Kamali, a member of parliament, heads the House of Workers. It was initially set up by the leftists after the revolution, and was later taken over by religious elements. It is sympathetic to the policies of the Tehran Combatant Clergy Association (breakaway group).

---

[7] Key figures in the Association are Hojatoleslam Mohammad Musavi-Kho'iniha, Hojatoleslam Ali Akbar Mohtashemi and Mehdi Karrubi, the former parliamentary speaker. This association broke off from the original ruling faction of the clergy (affiliated with President Rafsanjani), Majma'-e Rowhaniyat-e Mobarez-e Tehran, in the mid-1980's. A major point of contention between the factions is the extent and nature of the economic relations that Iran should have with Western countries. The breakaway faction completely opposes such links to the West. Members of the breakaway Association held the majority of seats in the Majlis, Iran's parliament, until the fourth parliamentary election in 1992. Prior to this election, many of the Association's candidates were rejected by the Council of Guardians on the ground that they were not qualified. The Association, however, still has a number of representatives in the Majlis and remains influential in determining state policy. See also footnote 4.

•*Tehran Times* (English-language) -- This paper, the continuation of a pre-revolutionary daily, is known to be associated with the policies of President Rafsanjani and the Foreign Ministry. It is published by the semi-autonomous foundation the Islamic Propagation Organization headed by Hojatoleslam Ahmad Jannati.[8]

•*Abrar* (Rightly Guided) -- This paper replaced the newspaper *Azadegan* (Liberated) after the government ordered it closed in 1985 for criticizing members of the Majlis. *Azadegan,* in the early revolutionary period, in turn had taken over the confiscated printing presses and premises of the left-wing newspaper *Ayandegan* (Futurists). It is published by Ghafur Garshassbi and is believed to be aligned with the Tehran Combatant Clergy Association (the breakaway group).

•*Resalat* (Prophetic Mission) -- This paper has been published since 1986. It follows a conservative pro-clergy line, sympathetic with President Rafsanjani's liberal economic policies but critical of his relatively liberal stance on social and cultural developments. It is owned by Hojatoleslam Ahmad Azari-Qomi, a prominent member of the Majlis.

•*Hamshahri* (Citizen) -- This paper is the latest addition to the list of daily newspapers and is distinguished by its use of color. It was launched by the mayor of Tehran, Gholam Hossain Karbaschi, in December 1992. It seems to voice the opinions of the more moderate factions within the political sphere.

In addition, there is one daily newspaper published in the provinces, *Khorasan,* which is distributed at a national level.

There are no dependable estimates of the daily circulation of individual papers. *Keyhan* is believed to be in the lead, followed by *Ettela'at,* both of them with circulations in the range of 100,000 to 300,000. But it is unclear how many of these two papers are actually read, since copies are distributed free to government offices. The remaining Persian daily newspapers claim a circulation of 20,000 to 40,000. The two English dailies have an estimated circulation of 5,000.

[8] Islamic Republic of Iran Broadcasting [hereinafter IRIB] Television First Program Network, June 22, 1992, as reported in FBIS, June 26, 1992.

In a recent report, the combined circulation of the national daily newspapers in Iran was estimated at less than one million--a small number in a country of about sixty million people.[9]

The national papers get imported newsprint from the government at a subsidized rate. Until recently, the government's subsidy was the difference between the official and free-market foreign exchange rates. Paper bought from the government at the official rate would be up to twenty times cheaper than paper bought at the free-market rate. Since March 1993, a single rate of foreign exchange has been implemented. The impact of this development on the situation of the press in Iran is uncertain, and much debated. For the time being, the government continues to provide paper to the newspapers at a subsidized rate, perpetuating official control.

Harassment of the Press

Although newspapers are all affiliated with various factions of the ruling elite, their editors and staff have not been immune from violent attack, government prosecution or censorship, especially when they have implicated the regime in a scandal or criticized state policy.

When the Islamic Republic News Agency (IRNA) recently criticized Iran's mass media for failure to counter "the enemy's information onslaught," an editorial in the newspaper *Salam* candidly identified three obstacles that the media face:

> Freedom in the writing of news reports . . . and the guarantee of job security is one of the important issues . . . . If the employees of the mass media have only a minimum of job security, where one report or article that is disapproved of can get an entire publication group fired, why should we expect people to want to join this profession? . . . There is also the issue of the forbidden realms of news. The fact that many questions are left hanging in mid-air without any answers by our officials means many issues remain covert and only filter through the foreign media . . . . [Public officials] believe that publications should merely be a personal bulletin (for the

[9] *Iran Times* (U.S.), January 1, 1993.

> officials) and not a strong modern institution for the service of society, the country and the people.[10]

In a number of instances, newspapers and their staff have been the victims of unchecked mob violence:

•In May 1993, a bomb exploded on the first floor of *Ettela'at*'s main office in Tehran.[11] No one claimed responsibility for the bomb, and the protesters' motive was obscure; but the attack is believed to be related to an incident about one month earlier, when a group attacked the office of *Ettela'at*-e *Haftegi*, its subsidiary weekly magazine, breaking windows. The protestors in that instance objected to the picture of a Revolutionary Guard who had died in the war with Iraq; it accompanied an article titled, "I have lost my mind."

•On August 26, 1991, Amin Sepehri, journalist for *Abrar*, was briefly detained, shorn and dragged through the streets of Pars-Abad in Eastern Azerbaijan with a rope around his neck on the orders of the local judiciary and the governor for allegedly "having implicated the local authorities in a financial scandal" in an article. He had accused the governor and the Moghan authorities of favoritism in an agricultural transport deal.

In other instances, the government has prosecuted and imprisoned newspaper editors and journalists for the content of their writing. For example:

•On September 28, 1992, the provincial manager of *Keyhan* in East Azerbaijan and a reporter of that newspaper were arrested by order of the Governor of Tabriz, Najafi Azar, for reporting news that "offended" the Governor. *Keyhan* had reported on the discharge of the Governor of central Tabriz, Behrouz Fakhmi, for slapping a colonel of the disciplinary forces while on duty. Azar took this report as a personal offense because he had appointed Fakhmi, and sent two letters of protest to *Keyhan*. Following their publication, Azar ordered the arrest and detention of the

---

10 *Salam*, February 24, 1993, as reported in FBIS, March 10, 1993.

11 *Iran Times*, May 28, 1993, p. 1.

newspaper manager and the responsible reporter. The reporter was beaten while in custody, and then released on bail pending investigation of his case. As regards the manager, the government stated that the complaint of the newspaper's manager was being investigated, and that an effort was made "to avoid the violation of freedom of expression by the press."[12] The press's alleged crime, not that of the government, was under investigation.

On a number of occasions, the government has charged journalists with espionage for activity that appears to be related to the practice of journalism. Middle East Watch is aware of several foreign journalists harassed in this manner.[13] At least one Iranian has also faced espionage charges: in June 1992, Salman Heydari, a journalist for the newspapers *Salam*[14] and *Abrar,* was arrested on charges of espionage[15] and accused of giving "secret government documents" to certain European embassies. The charges did not specify how he had obtained secret documents or which embassies received these documents. His case was sent to the Islamic Revolutionary Court. The case may have grown out of the fact that in 1989, the journalist was stationed in Turkey, during which time he reportedly had requested a visa for the United States.

The government's application of the Press Law to newspapers has been limited to providing protection to certain persons and certain policies. A telling example is the government's application of the anti-

---

[12] Response of the Islamic Republic of Iran to the United Nations Commission on Human Rights, (U.N. Doc. E/CN.4/1993/41/Add.1), Feb. 1993 [hereinafter Iran Response to U.N. Feb. 1993], at para. 73.

[13] See also Chapter 4.

[14] In an encounter reflective of the role of newspapers in interfactional conflicts, *Salam,* in its preliminary response to the arrest, criticized *Keyhan* for its coverage of the arrest and defamation of the journalist. *Salam* also questioned the government's inaction toward *Keyhan* in view of Article 39 of the Constitution which provides: "Attacks against the honor and dignity of a person who is arrested, detained, jailed, or punished by law are prohibited in any form." London *Keyhan,* July 9, 1992, p. 2.

[15] *Iran Focus,* July-August 1992, Vol. 5, No. 7, p. 8; cited in Article 19, *Press Under the Moderates,* p. 12.

defamation provision. Article 23 of the Press Law provides that whenever a false or insulting statement appears in the press, the person or legal entity implicated may submit a written response within a month after publication of the original statement; and the newspaper or magazine responsible for the statement must publish the response in a print and location commensurate with the original statement. If a response is not published, the person or legal entity can file a complaint with the General Prosecutor. When false or offensive material is published, Article 23(3) of the Press Law entitles the General Prosecutor to issue an initial warning to a publication, and should that not succeed in securing publication of a letter of protest from the offended party, suspend the publication for a maximum of ten days and submit its case to the court. There are only two known instances in which the government has sought to apply its own laws against defamation.[16]

•The first case was the September 1992 prosecution of the provincial manager and reporter of *Keyhan* for "offending" the Governor of Tabriz, recounted above; in that case, the government defined defamation so broadly as to encompass reporting on social policy.

•The second case is the recent prosecution of the publisher of *Abrar*. On March 3, 1993, Ghafur Garshassbi, the publisher of *Abrar*, was summoned to the Magistrate's Court of Tehran for publishing allegedly libelous material that had led to complaints. That day, a press release issued by the Public Relations Office of the court said that the paper had repeatedly published materials with "unscrupulous allegations against persons sometimes followed by either subsequent denials or corrections by way of apology or reminder to readers or explanation." According to the Islamic Republic News Agency, the publisher previously had been warned against dissemination of such material.[17] Four months later, the nature of the charges against Garshassbi is not yet known.

---

[16] Human Rights Watch believes that libel and defamation laws should be narrowly drawn to deal with false attacks on individual reputation. They can never properly be invoked by governments or government officials to shield their policies from public criticism.

[17] IRNA, March 3, 1993, as reported in FBIS, March 5, 1993.

MAGAZINES

Scores of non-political and specialized magazines exist in Iran, dealing with such subjects as economics, literature, sports, transportation, technology and science. Unlike newspapers, some magazines are independent, but these are denied the favorable government treatment that includes the allotment of generous quantities of paper at the official exchange rate, and they have small circulations. Deprived of a significant role in the national newspapers, radio or television, Iranian intellectuals have turned to magazines as the principal medium for voicing opposition and dissent. While outright political statements are prohibited, a round table on another topic -- modernism, the state of Iranian writing or the transfer of technology, for example -- can serve as a cover for critical political and social commentary. There is, however, no protection against mob attacks on magazines, their staff and editors.

These attacks have sometimes occurred at the incitement of government officials or the invitation of the state-affiliated press. At all times the attackers have enjoyed immunity from government prosecution. Examples of such attacks are:

• On June 23, 1992, protestors appeared at the office of *Keyhan* to object to a sewing pattern published in its subsidiary women's magazine, *Zan-e-Ruz* (Modern Woman).[18] *Salam* depicted the protestors as 300 motorcycle riders who chanted slogans and trashed the newspaper facilities. In a markedly different version of the incident, *Keyhan* stated that fewer than fifteen persons came to the office to complain about the design. The pattern is a drawing of a woman modeling an Islamic dress. The demonstrators contended that in the folds of the dress appeared a profile of Ayatollah Khomeini, while to most, the claim was completely unfounded and puzzling. *Zan-e-Ruz* continues to be published.

The incident exemplified, for many observers, the interfactional fighting that shows through the vigilante groups' attacks on the press. For example, an editorial in *Abrar* stated: "Those at *Keyhan* who have approved of attacks on other publications must now understand that an oversight, intentional or otherwise, must be handled in a court of law and

---

[18] *Iran Times*, July 3, 1992, p. 16. The sewing pattern is reproduced below.

The sewing pattern appearing in *Zan-e Ruz* magazine.

not by vigilantes."[19] *Keyhan* is the newspaper most frequently associated with encouraging mob attacks on other press organs.

•In May 1992, a group of five men attacked the office of *Donya-ye Sokhan* (World of Words) and demanded to search the premises. The three staff members who were working in the magazine office at the time asked to see their official order. One of the five, in lieu of an order, pulled out a pistol and proceeded to lock the three employees in a room. All the files in the premises were gathered and placed under the computer in the main room and blown up. No one was injured as a result of the bomb, but it caused enough damage to force the closure of *Donya-ye Sokhan*'s office for four months, reappearing in September. The reason for the attack is not known. However, in an earlier issue of the magazine, an article had suggested that "martyrdom" was an inappropriate name for a boys' school. The magazine had also published the work of some exiled writers, some of whom had opposed the *fatwa* against Salman Rushdie.[20]

Another tool of government control over magazines is to suspend publication for varying periods:

•In January 1993, *Ava-ye Shomal* (The Sound of the North), a weekly magazine published in Rasht, was suspended by the Ministry of Culture and Islamic Guidance for the publication of a picture of a "half-nude" woman in its movie pages. The official responsible for the page was fired for "carelessness,"[21] though the director of the publication was not implicated in the incident. The picture was associated with the screening of the American film *Basic Instinct* -- an exceptionally daring movie in the Iranian environment.

•In March 1991, the ten-month-old radical monthly magazine *Bayan* was forced to suspend publication "temporarily" under pressure from religious

---

[19] Ibid.

[20] See Chapter 7.

[21] London *Keyhan*, January 21, 1993, as reported in FBIS, February 4, 1993.

conservatives. *Bayan* used to be published by the Tehran Combatant Clergy Association (breakaway group).[22]

On a number of occasions, vigilante attacks have been a precursor to state prosecution of magazine editors and responsible staff. The instances involving the magazines *Farad* and *Gardoon* are examples of such prosecution. The prosecutions of the editors-in-chief of both magazines before a jury in general courts mark the first applications of the Press Law since its passage in 1985, and are discussed in detail in Chapter 3.

The prosecution of the cartoonist associated with the *Farad* incident, however, deserves particular attention here, because it was conducted before the Islamic Revolutionary Courts and in violation of the Press Law. The treatment of the accused was arbitrarily harsh.

Prosecution of Cartoonist Manouchehr Karimzadeh

On April 11, 1992, the Ministry of Culture and Islamic Guidance banned the science magazine *Farad* and arrested Nasser Arabha, its editor-in-chief, and Manouchehr Karimzadeh, a cartoonist, for printing a cartoon that "insulted the founder of the Islamic Republic Imam Khomeini." Karimzadeh was held at Evin prison in Tehran pending his trial. He was tried before the Islamic Revolutionary Court without a jury, and sentenced to one year imprisonment. An especially disturbing

---

[22] Hojatoleslam Mohtashemi, a leading figure in the Association, attributed the "temporary or permanent" closure of the magazine to "obstruction" by the government, and added:

> If the government did not want a magazine or a newspaper to be published -- and I do not know up to what extent it can bring itself to prevent such activities when publications are established on the basis of the press law, and no power can and should prevent it -- and if the government wants to confront such publications, then it should be brave enough to say so and not resort to a series of activities to try to hide its intentions while it closes down the publication.

Salam, May 16, 1993, as reported in FBIS, May 28, 1993.

feature of this case is that, in complete disregard of his rights, at the end of his sentence, the Supreme Court required that Karimzadeh be "re-tried."

The offending cartoon appeared in the April 1992 issue of the magazine and depicted a bearded man playing soccer with an amputated hand and leg (see reproduction, below); the cartoon accompanied an article on the poor state of soccer in Iran.[23] For some the man resembled Ayatollah Khomeini. Article 27 of the Press Law provides: "On every occasion that a publication offends the leader of the Islamic Revolution, the Council of Leadership or sources of emulation, its license will be canceled and the editor and the writer of the material will be referred to and prosecuted by a court of competent jurisdiction." Article 6(8) extends the scope of this prohibition to offensive cartoons as well. The government removed all copies of the magazine from newsstands soon after its publication.

A number of protest rallies were held in front of the *Farad* office in Tehran, and also in Qom, both before and after the government's arrest of Arabha and Karimzadeh. In one such protest, demonstrators chanted: "The American publisher must be punished. The follower of Salman Rushdie must be punished. The last will of Imam Khomeini must be complied with."[24] The demonstrators insisted on stricter scrutiny of the print media and the maximum penalty for sacrilege -- the death sentence -- and sacked the office of the magazine.

Certain aspects of the prosecution of Karimzadeh, in contrast to that of the editor of *Farad*, remain shrouded in secrecy. The exact date of his trial is not known, except that it preceded the more publicized prosecution of Arabha in September 1992 before a general court and in the presence of a jury. Tried before the Islamic Revolutionary Court, Karimzadeh was sentenced to one year imprisonment and fifty lashes. He was also fined 50,000 tomans (approximately $300).

---

[23] It is not clear whether the image depicts a wounded man, or simply a man running with one leg bent and a hand obscured in motion.

[24] IRNA, April 13, 1992, as reported in FBIS, April 14, 1992.

The cartoon appearing in *Farad,* April 1992.

His lawyer appealed the court's ruling. In May 1993, in granting the request of the Islamic Revolutionary Prosecutor, the Supreme Court affirmed the original finding of guilt, "canceled" Karimzadeh's sentence (which he was almost through serving) and required that he be "re-tried."[25] A date for his retrial has not yet been set.

[25] *Iran Times*, May 14, 1993, p. 1.

3
SELECTIVE APPLICATION OF THE PRESS LAW

Passed in 1985, the Press Law has been applied for the prosecution of press offenses only twice, in 1992. The cases are described below. Not only were the prosecutions highly selective, but the government failed to act in accordance with the Press Law in the Maroufi case, in whose initial stages the Islamic Revolutionary Courts were used.

PROSECUTION OF NASSER ARABHA
FARAD

On April 11, 1992, the Ministry of Culture and Islamic Guidance -- on recommendation of its press council[1] -- banned the magazine *Farad* and ordered the arrest of Nasser Arabha, the editor-in-chief, and Manouchehr Karimzadeh,[2] a cartoonist, for printing a cartoon that "insulted the founder of the Islamic Republic Imam Khomeini." Arabha was held at the notorious Evin prison in Tehran pending trial. His arrest followed mass vigilante attacks on the *Farad* office in Tehran, demonstrations in Qom and instances where protesters called for the application of the death sentence to Arabha.

The editor's trial was held on September 16, 1992, before Branch 2 of the Criminal Court in Tehran, where he was represented by counsel. He was charged with "acting against internal security and insulting the exalted Imam Khomeini." He denied the charge but admitted negligence. He was tried and convicted by a seven-person jury,[3] but the jury recommended leniency in view of his "cultural services" and lack of

---

[1] See Chapter 1 for discussion of the press council.

[2] For the prosecution of Manouchehr Karimzadeh, see Chapter 2.

[3] The seven-person jury consisted of: Ayatollah Mohagegh Damad (*Faqih*), Ata'ollah Mohajerani (Assistant to the President for parliamentary and legal affairs), Goodarz Eftekhar-Jahromi (Advisor to the President), Jalal Rafi' (Editor-in-Chief of *Ettela'at*), Ayatollah Mohammad Taqi Fazel-Meybodi (*Faqih*), Ahmad Purnejati (academic), Mohammad Javad Sahebi (Editor-in-Chief of *Keyhan Andisheh*).

knowledge of the cartoon. His case is the first press violation tried by a jury before the general courts.

A number of hard-line newspapers, notably *Jomhouri-ye Islami* and *Keyhan*, criticized the judiciary for its "lenient" sentence in the case of *Farad*. By contrast, the Rafsanjani-aligned *Tehran Times*, in reference to mass attacks on the *Farad* facilities and protesters' demand for the execution of the editor, observed: "[I]f the people are to implement punishments in these cases, this will simply bring about chaos and anarchy, debilitate the judicial power, and rob the mass media officials of job security."[4]

Arabha was sentenced to six months in prison and released in early 1993 upon completion of his sentence.[5] The magazine remains banned.

PROSECUTION OF ABBAS MAROUFI
GARDOON

Abbas Maroufi, editor-in-chief of the literary and cultural monthly *Gardoon*, was charged with anti-Islamic offenses and tried before a jury in the general courts in December 1992. His trial was remarkable both for the rare application of the largely dormant Press Law of 1985 and for his acquittal. Nevertheless, the string of events leading up to and subsequent to the trial illustrate the persistent extrajudicial and erratic workings of censorship and government control.

The August 1992 issue of the magazine was devoted to the topic of returning Iranian emigrants. It carried a cover illustration by Parviz Kalantari, depicting a woman in Islamic garb lying motionless on the ground while a plane resembling a tie (symbolizing the West) passed overhead (see reproduction, below). *Keyhan* reacted to this particular issue by attacking the cover design as being anti-*hejab*,[6] and issued a public invitation to Muslim women to respond, in an August 8 article

---

[4] IRNA, June 27, 1992, as reported in FBIS, July 2, 1992.

[5] *Iran Times*, May 14, 1993, p. 1.

[6] *Hejab* refers to the Islamic head cover which is now mandatory for women in Iran.

The cover design of *Gardoon,* August 1992

titled, "Is everyone asleep?"[7]

On August 10, ten woman attacked the offices of *Gardoon* and demanded that it be closed down because of its offensive cover illustration. When asked to present their official order, the woman at the head of the group pulled out a pistol and stated that they were representing *Hozeih Honari Sazman Tabligat Islami* (Art Center for the Islamic Propagation Organization), an influential semi-autonomous foundation. The woman at the head of the group was A. Saghfi, a writer for *Keyhan*.

A few days after this incident, the Islamic Revolutionary Court summoned Maroufi, and asked him to deliver orders to twelve persons[8] who had previously written for *Gardoon* to present themselves to the Court. Maroufi refused to deliver the orders. On October 9, after printing the twentieth issue of *Gardoon*, the magazine was banned by order of the Islamic Revolutionary Court in Tehran. This order was in violation of Article 12 of the Press Law which authorizes the press council, and not the Islamic Revolutionary Court, to pursue press offenses.

Maroufi was indicted by the Islamic Revolutionary Prosecutor. As reprinted in the Iranian newspaper, *Jomhouri-ye Islami*, the bill of indictment prepared by the Islamic Revolutionary Prosecutor charged Maroufi with "presenting ways and directives on how to oppose the holy system of the Islamic Republic of Iran; spreading rumors against the holy system and its officials; insulting the Islamic Republic of Iran and its officials; insulting the lofty position of clericalism; insulting the precept of sacred defense; insulting the *Hezbollah*; and propagandizing and propagating a vile monarchical culture."[9]

In November, Maroufi was attacked on the street as he was leaving the *Gardoon* offices by two men in civilian clothes who called him by name. His attackers pinned him to the wall and accused him of being a drug smuggler, stating that they represented the Anti-Narcotics Section

---

[7] *Keyhan*, August 8, 1992.

[8] Ten of the persons summoned were: Abdolhassan Nahifi, Mohammad Ali Sepanloo, Parviz Kalantari, Fereshteh Sari, Simin Behbahani, Manouchehr Kohan, Karim Kouchizadeh, Farokh Tamimi, Mehdi Sahabi and himself.

[9] December 16, 1992, as reported in FBIS, January 7, 1993.

of the Islamic Revolutionary Prosecutor's Office.[10] When a crowd gathered, the two men departed.

Maroufi's one-day trial was held at the First Criminal Court of Tehran (Branch 135) on December 8, 1992. Pursuant to Article 34 of the Press Law, a jury was present -- a jury composed largely of Maroufi's professional peers from the state-affiliated press.[11] Maroufi was represented by legal counsel, and the jury found him not guilty of press offenses.[12] In so finding, the jury significantly stated: "Although the articles printed in *Gardoon*, as cited in the bill of indictment, were not at times in line with the aspirations of the Islamic revolution, they did not constitute a legal crime."[13] The court therefore acquitted Maroufi and allowed the magazine to resume publication.

All preliminary stages of Maroufi's prosecution, up to the point of trial, were in violation of the Press Law. In issuing its verdict, the court acknowledged this fact by stating that the Revolutionary Prosecutor's bill of indictment lacked a date and file number, and that the bill itself violated Article 12 of the Press Law.

Although acquitted, Maroufi was unable to renew publication of *Gardoon* immediately after trial as provided by the court's order and Article 7(a) of the Press Law. In fact, after his trial, a government official from the Ministry of Culture and Islamic Guidance called Maroufi and asked him not to publish his magazine until after the Iranian New Year in March 1993, since the *javv* was not appropriate because of "*hezbollahi* pressure groups." Should he choose to publish *Gardoon* before this time, the official notified Maroufi, the Ministry "could not be responsible for your life." *Gardoon* resumed publication in April 1993.

---

[10] Prior to this incident, Maroufi had contacts with the Anti-Narcotics Section for press-related issues. He was summoned to the Anti-Narcotics Section in May 1991 and questioned about his writings on the topic of a writers' syndicate. He responded to their inquiries by stating that such matters were not within the jurisdiction of the Anti-Narcotics Section. The officials urged him to take their remarks as "advice."

[11] The composition of the jury was the same as in the prosecution of Nasser Arabha. See footnote 3.

[12] The court's verdict of acquittal was upheld on appeal in March 1993.

[13] Text as translated by Middle East Watch.

4
FOREIGN MEDIA AND JOURNALISTS

The means of government control over the foreign media are similar to those that govern the domestic press, largely based on the threat of reprisal after publication. Reprisals for "undesirable" news stories have included closure of local offices of foreign news agencies, expulsion or imprisonment of foreign journalists, and harassment or imprisonment of Iranian journalists who work for foreign news agencies.

Foreign journalists' access to Iran was restricted soon after the revolution. The newly constituted Islamic Republic of Iran expelled foreign journalists and closed local offices of news agencies on the assertion that their reporting was "biased and false." This was ironic, given that foreign journalists had played a significant role in promoting and shaping the revolution -- as news of escalating events inside Iran was transmitted beyond its borders, the words of Ayatollah Khomeini were carried from his new place of exile in Paris to Iran by numerous foreign radio stations.[1] Since the end of the Iran-Iraq war, however, restrictions on foreign journalists have decreased.

The Central Office for Foreign Press and Publications (*Edareh Kol Matbooat va Rasanehay Khareji*) of the Ministry of Culture and Islamic Guidance supervises the activities of foreign journalists and Iranians working for foreign news agencies. It is also responsible for issuing the permit necessary for establishing a permanent office.

WORKING CONDITIONS

Iranian journalists working for foreign news agencies are the most vulnerable to government pressure. They are often "summoned" to the Ministry of Culture and Islamic Guidance, questioned and held accountable for the reports of their affiliated foreign news agency. Iranian journalists also enjoy far less latitude in reporting than do their

---

[1] With the outbreak of protests against the Shah in 1978, many foreign journalists were sent to Iran to cover the revolution and subsequent events; by the beginning of 1980, there were more than 300 foreign correspondents from twenty-six countries working in Iran. *Index on Censorship*, June 1980, p. 65.

foreign colleagues.[2] For fear of further reprisal, Iranian journalists do not publicize incidents of harassment, while the treatment of foreign journalists often receives international coverage. The government, acutely aware of the impact of foreign news, generally treats foreign journalists well once they are allowed to enter the country.

Treatment of Iranian journalists working for foreign news agencies at times extends beyond harassment and questioning. They risk losing their journalist cards,[3] temporarily or permanently, which has significant financial implications. They also face imprisonment, sometimes without being charged with any offense. For example:

• Jahangir Jahanbagloo, an Iranian freelance journalist, has been working for foreign news agencies and television networks over the past eleven years. He has been the official representative of the American television network NBC since April 1991. In November 1992, however, he was summoned to the Ministry of Culture and Islamic Guidance and informed that henceforth his accreditation was canceled. The representative of the Ministry stated that he was acting on orders and didn't know the reasons for the cancellation. Since November, Jahanbagloo has pursued his case with various officials within the Ministry and inquired about the reasons for cancelling his journalist card but to no avail. Official responses have been varied and arbitrary, ranging from "You did not work within the framework," to "We acted upon orders from above," to "You must have contacted persons you shouldn't have contacted." In March 1993, Jahanbagloo wrote a letter to the head of the Ministry stating that his basic rights had been denied and, once again, requesting to know the reasons for cancelling his card. The government has not responded to his letter. The financial consequences

---

[2] An example of the disparate treatment of Iranian journalists involves the transportation of film and video out of Iran. For Iranian journalists, the government demands to have the film developed and to see the video before issuing an exit permit (see the case of Kaveh Golestan below). Foreign journalists generally are not subject to the same restrictions.

[3] Any Iranian journalist who works for a foreign news agencies or television networks must have his journalist card approved by the Ministry of Intelligence before it is issued by the Ministry of Culture and Islamic Guidance. Other Iranian journalists generally are not required to get this approval.

of the government's arbitrary interference with his ability to pursue his profession have been serious.

• Bahram Molaie is an Iranian freelance cameraman who has worked for a number of foreign television networks, including the American CBS and ABC networks, in Iran. In August 1987, when he had returned to Iran to cover a news story, he was interrogated by the Ministry of Intelligence about his work; his journalist card was taken from him, and he was asked to sign a declaration that he would not leave the country until further notice. Subsequently, officials confiscated his passport. In March 1988, without being charged with any offense, he was arrested by the Islamic Revolutionary Prosecutor and imprisoned for forty-five days in Evin Prison in Tehran without trial. It was not until long after he was released from prison that the Islamic Revolutionary Prosecutor's Office notified him, in late 1991, that the reason for his investigation and imprisonment was the "suspicion of espionage," but, since there was nothing in his file, it was now closed. Molaie was later allowed to travel outside of the country, yet he has been unable to recover his journalist card and is still barred from working in his profession in Iran.

Foreign news agencies with local offices are more vulnerable to government pressure and harassment than visiting foreign journalists, and their employees have also on occasion been summoned to the Ministry in response to "undesirable" news stories. Agence France-Presse (AFP) is the only leading Western news agency operating out of Tehran. The other news agencies with permanent offices in Tehran include: New China News Agency (China), Anatolia (Turkey), ANSA (Italy), Tass (Russia), SANA (Syria), JANA (Libya) and WAFA (Palestine News Agency). The Japanese Asahi, Kiyoda, Yomiuri and NHK-TV news agencies also have permanent representatives.

The government uses visas as the means to control other foreign journalists. Chris Hedges, *The New York Times*'s Middle East correspondent, told Middle East Watch that the issuance of visas is based on a system of "reward and punishment."[4] The government refuses to issue visas to journalists, some temporarily and others permanently, whose past work it does not like. A French correspondent, when she applied in early 1993 for a visa to follow up on a visit made last year, was

---

[4] Middle East Watch interview, July 1, 1993.

told by an official at the Iranian Embassy: "We don't like your work. You are not fair. You are not kind to us. We won't give you a visa. You will have to wait for months and months." Despite this admonition, she was invited to visit Iran in February 1993 for President Rafsanjani's press conference, and returned once again in June 1993 to cover the presidential elections.

Visas, however, do not always guarantee that the journalist will be allowed into the country. For example, in February 1993, Chris Hedges was given a five-day visa to attend President Rafsanjani's press conference. Once he arrived at the airport, his passport was taken from him and he was detained at the airport overnight and denied phone calls. Early the next morning, he was expelled to Turkey. The Iranian government attributed the incident to the fact that the officials at the airport were concerned about the "authenticity" of his visa. Subsequently, Hedges visited Iran in June for two weeks.

Once foreign journalists arrive in Tehran, they are required to check in with the Ministry of Culture and Islamic Guidance and leave their addresses. Movement within Tehran is unrestricted. One journalist recently told Middle East Watch, "You jump into a taxi and go wherever you want and speak with whomever you want." Meeting with certain government officials, however, is not easy. Photojournalists or cameramen are more likely to attract the attention of local authorities and to be questioned about their activities. Journalists who require the assistance of translators are also more subject to official control. Translators must be approved by the Ministry of Culture and Islamic Guidance and are often employees of the Ministry itself.

Movement outside of Tehran, however, is strictly monitored. In order to leave Tehran, journalists must obtain written permission from the Ministry, which in most cases means being accompanied by a representative of the Ministry. There may be adverse consequences to traveling without a permit:

•In his June 1993 visit, Hedges traveled to Nowshahr on the Caspian Sea without permission; he was arrested, detained for five hours and ordered to return to Tehran.

•In June 1993, two Dutch journalists left Tehran without a permit from the Ministry. With the assistance of two foreign friends as translators, they traveled by taxi for four days. On their return to Tehran, they were met at their hotel by officials from the Ministry of Intelligence who had been looking for them during their absence. The Iranian taxi driver was taken away, interrogated about the places they had visited and people they had spoken with, and later released.

Due to the lack of centralized control in Iran, some foreign journalists have discovered that their written permission was not sufficient for local authorities. The areas bordering Iraq are particularly sensitive. By contrast, visiting other places, such as the historical and cultural city of Isfahan, is actively promoted by the government.

The movement of foreign journalists and their access to information were more closely monitored during the Iran-Iraq war. Reporting on the war could lead to expulsion and detention:

•In January 1987, Gerald Seib, the Middle East bureau chief of the *Wall Street Journal,* was arrested in Tehran, detained for six days and then released.[5] He was accused of being a "spy of the US, Israel and Iraq" during his ten-day stay in the country. Seib was one of fifty foreign journalists invited by the Iranian authorities to report on the Iranian military offensive in the Iran-Iraq war.

•On July 13, 1986, Hugh Pope, a Reuters correspondent, was expelled on the accusation that he had revealed military secrets in a dispatch concerning an Iraqi raid on a satellite communication station.[6]

Political factors can affect the treatment accorded foreign journalists. In a number of instances, the Iranian authorities have retaliated against adverse policies implemented by foreign governments by expelling journalists working for that country's news media. For example:

•On February 20, 1990, the Ministry of Culture and Islamic Guidance revoked the accreditation of the Iranian stringer working for the British Broadcasting Corporation in Tehran, in reprisal for the British

---

[5] *Index on Censorship*, March 1987, p. 38.

[6] *Index on Censorship*, August 1986, p. 38.

government's deportation of nine Iranians, including the head of the Iranian radio and television bureau in London.[7]

•At the end of February 1986, the authorities expelled four Frenchmen, including Jacques Charmelot, the AFP correspondent in Tehran.[8] Although the authorities charged them with "spying" for Iraq, it is believed that the expulsions were a response to the expulsion by France of two Iranians and two Iraqi dissidents close to Iran.

While foreign journalists' access to Iran has improved since the Iran-Iraq war, the resignation of the former Minister of Culture and Islamic Guidance, Mohammad Khatami, has meant new restrictions for some journalists. One foreign reporter told Middle East Watch that for the group associated with Khatami's successor, Ali Larijani, once again "foreign journalists are the equivalent of spies." Foreign journalists in general, however, find working conditions in Iran more favorable than in some other countries in the region, such as Iraq and Syria, and one Iranian working for a foreign news agency told Middle East Watch that in the past year the Ministry's treatment of foreign press had become more professional and less confrontational -- while adding that these improvements applied only to foreign, and not domestic, media.

Foreign Publications

Under Article 22 of the Press Law, foreign printed matter entering the country must accord with "religious norms, the Constitution and the system of the Islamic Republic." Such foreign newspapers and magazines as the *Financial Times*, *Der Spiegel*, *Time* and *Newsweek* therefore can be purchased at Tehran newsstands, but only after the Ministry of Culture and Islamic Guidance has approved their content. For example, the February 19 and March 12, 1990 issues of *Newsweek* were banned from distribution due to their coverage of the Israeli politician Ariel

[7] IRNA, February 20, 1990, as reported in FBIS, February 20, 1990.

[8] *Index on Censorship*, May 1986, p. 39.

Sharon and the gay movement in the United States.[9] The May 18, 1993 issue of *Der Spiegel* was banned because it contained an interview with Salman Rushdie.[10] Additionally, the expensive price and limited circulation of these periodicals limit their reach.[11]

PUBLIC ACCESS TO INTERNATIONAL NEWS

Official international news broadcasts in Iran are placed within the framework of cultural domination, Western imperialism and national struggles for independence and non-alignment. Official reports emphasize primarily the Arab and Islamic world, and secondarily the underdeveloped and colonized world. Despite the anti-Western rhetoric of the Islamic Republic, however, its news agencies rely significantly on the major Western news agencies; one study estimated that Western news agencies supplied sixty-one percent of all foreign stories.[12] Foreign radio broadcasts, moreover, provide an important, unofficial source of news (see Chapter 5).

Iranian newspapers, radio and television primarily access international news through state-affiliated agencies. The most common source of foreign news is the Islamic Republic News Agency (IRNA), which is a part of the Ministry of Culture and Islamic Guidance. IRNA provides news through its own representatives in thirty countries. It also serves as an intermediary for news from foreign news agencies to the

---

[9] IRNA, February 19, 1990, reported in FBIS, February 20, 1990; and Committee to Protect Journalists, *Attacks on the Press 1990: A Worldwide Survey* (New York: 1991), p. 59.

[10] Reporters Sans Frontières, *1993 Report*, (Hampshire, U.K.: 1993), p. 151.

[11] One study in 1989 estimated that 500 copies of *Time* and *Newsweek* were distributed in Iran on a weekly basis. Iran Research Group, *Iran Yearbook 89/90* (Bonn: MB Median, 1989), p. 21-29.

[12] Pirouz Shoar-Ghaffari, "News of the Outside World in the Post-Revolutionary Iranian Press," *Gazette* (Netherlands), 1991, pp. 1-18.

local press. In the past, due to an unrealistic official exchange rate,[13] the local press could not afford to buy news directly from foreign news agencies in foreign currency and instead would purchase news from IRNA in Iranian currency. The recent merging of the three separate foreign exchange rates into one rates may alter this practice. Voice and Vision of the Islamic Republic of Iran, the government radio and television network, also has its own representatives abroad.

A Banned Journalist
Kaveh Golestan

Kaveh Golestan, an Iranian photojournalist well known for his work on the 1979 revolution and the Iran-Iraq war, has been prevented from leaving Iran and from working since June 1992. The reason is a film made in Iran and screened abroad with the full approval and knowledge of the Ministry of Culture and Islamic Guidance. With the constantly changing tide, or *javv*, and internecine conflicts, previously-obtained permits have provided him no protection against government arbitrariness and abuse. More than a year since the investigation against him began, Golestan still awaits disposition of his case.

Golestan was commissioned by the United Kingdom's Channel 4 TV program *South*[14] to produce a film on Iran. After consultation with the Ministry, Golestan started work in January 1991 describing the situation of journalists working in Iran. The twenty-seven-minute film, *Recording the Truth,* brought together Iranian journalists from a variety of political and social backgrounds and solicited their views on freedom of expression, the universality of human rights principles, and democracy. This endeavor provided a rare and untainted glimpse into the world of journalists working in Iran who took positions for and against the policies of the government. Significantly, most work on the film occurred during the period of relatively enhanced freedom of expression under former Minister of Culture and Islamic Guidance Mohammad Khatami.

---

[13] See Chapter 2 for discussion of different exchange rates.

[14] *South* specializes on issues in the developing world as portrayed by persons native to such countries.

Prior to release, the film was viewed and the accuracy of its content approved by all who had participated in it. As previously agreed, Golestan also submitted a copy of the unedited version to the Ministry, along with a request for permission to take the film abroad. The Ministry did not respond to this request for over six weeks, despite numerous inquires by Golestan. In order to secure a permit to export the film in time to meet his contractual obligations, Golestan obtained the assistance of Hojatoleslam Mohammad-Ali Zam who heads the Hozeih Honari Sazman Tabligath Islami (Art Center of the Islamic Propagation Organization), an influential semi-autonomous foundation.

The film was first presented on December 14, 1991 on the *South* program and was made available at the Rotterdam Film Festival in January 1992. Additionally, a full translated transcript of the film appeared in the March 1992 issue of *Index on Censorship*. The political climate in Iran, however, had undergone a significant change since the previous year, marked by Khatami's resignation on May 24, 1992 and its acceptance by President Rafsanjani on July 14.

Since his return to Iran in June 1992, Golestan has been unable to leave the country. Within days of arriving in Tehran, he was summoned to appear before the Islamic Revolutionary Prosecutor's Office. On July 14, 1992, Golestan was served with a summons.

The next day, he presented himself to the officials at the Revolutionary Prosecutor's Office and was interrogated by representatives of that office and of the Ministry of Intelligence. Before being released that afternoon, he was required to sign a declaration that he would not leave the country. Even travel outside the capital must be approved by the government, with the possibility that he be accompanied by an official. His journalist work permit has been cancelled "pending further investigation and disposition of his case."

All the journalists featured in the film were also questioned and then released by the Revolutionary Prosecutor's Office in February 1992. After questioning, they were instructed to cease all contact with Golestan. Although not subject to any official sanction, they are experiencing much difficulty in having their work accepted by newspapers and magazines.

Since his interrogation, an official from the Revolutionary Prosecutor's Office has been assigned to Golestan's case. The official has informed him verbally of questions "critical" to the investigation and directed that he respond to them in writing. The only paper trail that exists involves statements in Golestan's own handwriting. Golestan has consistently maintained that he has not violated any law.

In testimony to the complexity and contradiction that shape the day-to-day existence of artists and intellectuals in Iran, last fall after having been stripped of his journalist card and barred from leaving Tehran, Golestan was asked by the government to teach at the Arts College at the University of Tehran. In hopes that this would assist the resolution of the government's investigation, he accepted the position. But little has been done to end the unlawful and arbitrary official interference with his life and profession.

5
STATE-CONTROLLED RADIO AND TELEVISION

In a country that is forty-eight percent illiterate, radio and television are critical forms of communication. The Islamic regime places these media under the direct supervision of the religious leader and the three branches of government. Article 175 of the Constitution reads in relevant part:

> The appointment and dismissal of the head of the Radio and Television of the Islamic Republic of Iran rests with the Leader. A council consisting of two representatives each of the President, the head of the judiciary branch and the Islamic Consultative Assembly shall supervise the functioning of this organization.

The Constitution's Preamble requires that the mass media "must strictly refrain from diffusion and propagation of destructive and anti-Islamic practices," and exclusively serve the views of the prevailing ideology.

Radio and television programs have the advantage of reaching a large number of people; there are an estimated 5,250,000 TV sets in Iran.[1] The mass appeal of their programs, however, is limited by their lack of diversity and largely political and religious content. Of the two radio networks that transmit nationwide, Radio Network 1 broadcasts a mix of news reports, talks, speeches and non-vocal music; Radio Network 2 primarily broadcasts parliamentary debate, Friday prayer sermons and religious teachings. There are also two TV channels. Channel 1 covers ninety percent of the country, and Channel 2, sixty-five percent. TV programs primarily consist of news reports, competitions, Islamic ideology courses, and political programs.[2] A third TV channel was expected to start operating in 1993, covering sixty percent of the country, but so far has not begun broadcasting.[3]

---

[1] Deborah Young, "Iranian Cinema Now," *Variety International Film Guide*, 1993, p. 29.

[2] Iran Research Group, *Iran Yearbook*, p. 21-28.

[3] *Iran Times*, February 26, 1993, p. 2.

No voice other than that of the government finds a place in the radio and television. Even contentious discourse from within government circles is not broadcast. For example, on October 3, 1991, the direct emission of the parliamentary debate on the radio was abruptly cut off when the debate between partisans of Ayatollah Khamenei and other factions within the Majlis became heated.[4]

Deviation from the government line carries penalties. On January 29, 1989, for example, Ayatollah Khomeini was deeply offended by a radio interview in which a woman stated that her role model was not the daughter of the prophet Mohammad but a Japanese TV soap-opera star. As a result, the persons responsible for the emission were punished. The broadcast director at the Tehran radio, Mohammad Arab Mazar-Yazdi, was sentenced to five years in jail.[5] Three directors of the in-house "Islamic ideology group" were sentenced to four years each. All four were also sentenced to fifty lashes. On February 2, Ayatollah Khomeini granted amnesty to all four.[6]

Mass media traditionally have been placed under the supervision of "insiders." During the Shah's last decade in power, Reza Qotbi, the cousin of Queen Farah, was in charge of the radio and television. Immediately after the revolution, Sadeq Qotbzadeh, the main spokesman for Ayatollah Khomeini in Paris, assumed this position until he was executed for "plotting against the revolution and against Islam." Mohamad Hashemi, the brother of President Rafsanjani, is presently in charge of the radio and television network, the Voice and Vision of the Islamic Republic of Iran.

Technology, however, poses a significant threat to the government's campaign to control information and images through the control of the mass media. Satellite communication and radio broadcasts serve as conduits for the "onslaught" of foreign values and anti-revolutionary propaganda which jeopardize the supremacy of the Islamic

---

4 Reporters Sans Frontières, *1991 Report* (Hampshire, U.K.: 1991), p. 95.

5 *The New York Times*, February 10, 1989.

6 *Le Monde*, February 3, 1989.

system.[7] For the most part, these media lie outside the government's control. Although the use of satellites is prohibited, there are an unknown number of satellite dishes in Iran. Moreover, large numbers tune in to foreign radios for news.[8] Recognizing the government's inability to block these channels of exchange, the Minister of Interior Hojatoleslam Abdollah Nuri stated on December 10, 1992:

> Cultural issues are of great importance because we cannot repulse TV and radio waves transmitted from alien countries. Rather, we should act in such a manner that if people are to choose between foreign TV programs and ours, our programs will be their choice. This is not possible unless we enhance our publicity capability.[9]

A number of political opposition groups forced to continue their struggles in exile dispatch radio programs to Iran. Below we provide a partial listing of these clandestine radio broadcasts, their political affiliation and their place of transmission. The government has been more successful in jamming broadcasts by Iranian opposition groups, which tend to have relatively weak transmission, than foreign government-owned radios. Border provinces such as Kurdistan and Khuzestan more easily receive these programs, due to their transmission from neighboring Iraq or Egypt.

Foreign television broadcasts reaching the border provinces of Iran from neighboring countries such as Iraq, Turkey and Azerbaijan also provide an alternative to government television. Iraqi state television

---

[7] There also exists a lively black market in illegal music cassettes and videos (see Chapter 8).

[8] The numerous foreign radio broadcasts to Iran in Persian include: Voice of America (twenty-eight hours per week), Radio Moscow (twenty-one), BBC (sixteen and one-half), Voice of Turkey (fourteen), Radio Cairo (fourteen), Saudi Arabia Broadcasting Service (fourteen), Deutsche Welle (eleven hours and forty minutes) Radio France International (seven), Trans World Radio (five and one-half) and Radio Israel (five).

[9] IRNA, December 10, 1992, as reported in FBIS, December 11, 1992.

broadcasts also include a weekly program by the People's Mojahedin Khalq of Iran, an armed opposition movement.

Partial List of Clandestine Radio Broadcasts to Iran

•*Seda-ye Kurdistan Iran* (Voice of Iranian Kurdistan). Organization: Kurdish Democratic Party of Iran. Broadcast from Iraq. In Persian and Kurdish.

•*Seda-ye Engelab-e Iran* (Voice of the Iranian Revolution). Organization: Iranian Communist Party (Kurdish wing). Broadcast from Iraq. In Persian and Kurdish.

•*Seda-ye Kurdistan Iran, Rahbari Engelabi* (Voice of Iranian Kurdistan, Revolutionary Leadership). Organization: Kurdish Democratic Party of Iran (Revolutionary Leadership). Broadcast from Iraq. In Persian and Kurdish.

•*Seda-ye Mojahed* (Voice of the Mojahed). Organization: People's Mojahedin Khalq of Iran. Broadcast from Iraq. In Persian.

•*Radio-Azadi* (Radio Freedom). Organization: National Resistance Movement of Iran. Broadcast from Egypt. In Persian.

•*Seda-ye Jonbesh-e Mojahedin-e Baluchestan-e Iran* (Voice of the Crusaders of Iranian Baluchestan). Organization: Crusaders of Iranian Baluchestan. Broadcast from Iraq. In Baluchi.

•*Seda-ye Hoquq-e Bashar va Aazadi-ye Iran* (Voice of Human Rights and Freedom for Iran). Organization: Human Rights and Freedom for Iran (Previously Flag of Freedom). Broadcast from Egypt. In Persian.

6
BOOK PUBLISHING

At first glance, the Iranian regime does not appear to oppose the circulation of ideas through books. The number of published book titles has increased notably since the pre-revolutionary era, while still remaining at modest levels in a country of approximately sixty million people. One study estimates that 2,777 books were published in 1976 and 4,810 books in 1987.[1] Religious texts constitute a significant portion of books published since 1979, estimated at twenty-five percent in 1990.[2] Similarly, there has been a significant rise in circulation; the average number of print runs for a book is presently around 3,000, as compared to 1,000 to 2,000 before 1979.[3] The government stated in a report to UNESCO that 2,993 book titles entered their first printing in 1992, with a total circulation of 24,309,000.[4] The quantity may obscure the fact that the content of these books is controlled.

Of prime interest are books relating to revolutionary experiences in general and that of Iran in particular. Translations of such books often present little political difficulty to Iranian writers and publishers and, for this reason, are quite popular endeavors.[5] The works of Western philosophers, sociologists, political scientists and literary figures are also widely available in translation. Compared to the pre-revolutionary period, there is a more diverse pool of translated work,

---

[1] Mehrzad Boroujerdi, "Intellectuals, Literature and Publishing Houses in Iran: 1960-1990." Paper presented at the annual meeting of the Middle East Association, San Antonio, Texas, November 1990.

[2] *Adineh* (Iran), April 1990, p. 97.

[3] Mahmood Tolooi, "Tirage, Kamiyat ya Kayfiyat?" (Circulation, Quantity or Quality?) *Donya-ye Sokhan* (Iran), February/March 1992, p. 50.

[4] *Iran Times*, May 7, 1993, p. 5.

[5] These books include U.S. Ambassador William Sullivan's *Mission to Iran*, Hamilton Jordan's *Crisis*, Pierre Salinger's *America Held Hostage*, and James Bill's *The Eagle and the Lion*. Significantly, similar endeavors authored by Iranians often are banned, such as the Shah's *Answer to History*, Fereidun Hoveyda's *The Fall of the Shah*, and Hushang Nahavandi's *Two Broken Dreams* and *Anatomy of a Revolution*.

including Arab, African and Latin American authors. In the period of 1986-1990, Iran experienced a dramatic 355-percent increase in the importation of books, primarily by English- and French-language publishers.[6]

An annual International Book Fair, held in Tehran since 1988, brings foreign books and publishers to Iran. The regulations of the Fair require that foreign publishers comply with the moral standards of the Islamic Republic of Iran: "Books with obscene images, anti-religious and anti-Islamic works, as well as all works that propagate Zionism and racial discrimination are forbidden."[7] The Sixth Book Fair in May 1993 was attended by representatives of 320 foreign publishing houses. Of these, fifty-three were American and seventy-three British,[8] but bilateral tensions between Iran and the U.S. and British governments, over the Salman Rushdie affair and other issues, meant that they were represented at the fair by their Iranian agents. French and German publishers did not take part in the book fair at all because of the Rushdie affair. Arab countries, namely Libya, Egypt and Syria, had a significant constituency at the Fair.[9] Due to strained government relations, Egypt was also represented by Iranian agents.

Censorship is pervasive, however. Nearly three-fourths of the books published in Iran are funded by the state or state-aligned foundations.[10] And through a range of formal and informal mechanisms, the government censors books -- because they are popular and not in accord with the prevailing ideology, or because their authors' very identity is considered "counter-revolutionary," as in the case of writers who have opposed the regime's excesses. To evade the official controls, there is a lively exchange of photocopied banned books and poetry that circulate underground at inflated prices.

---

[6] *Le Monde*, March 26, 1992, p. 28.

[7] Ibid.

[8] *Libération* (Morocco), May 7, 1993, p. 2; *Iran Times*, May 14, 1993, p. 2; and *Iran Times*, May 21, 1993, p.2

[9] *Libération*, May 7, 1993, p. 2.

[10] See discussion below in this chapter.

The Scope of Censorship

The thousands of years of Iranian history have produced a particularly rich literary tradition. But the "seditious" written word does not seriously endanger the official value system, for nearly half of the population is illiterate, and avid readers constitute a minority. Since the summer of 1991, moreover, book sales have been on the decline due to their rising cost and generally difficult economic conditions. The relatively few volumes published per print run, and exorbitant prices for books, additionally hinder their distribution. Particularly in the case of controversial books that appear in the market from time to time, as one Iranian writer told Middle East Watch, they serve only to "preach to the converted."

There is no comprehensive listing of banned books or writers; the government rarely issues formal banning orders. The remarkable exception is the Ministry of Culture and Islamic Guidance's November 1992 order banning all the works of two poets residing in exile, Nader Naderpour and Esmail Khoei, in reprisal for their publicly stating their opposition to the Salman Rushdie *fatwa*.[11] As a general rule, publishers often are informally and verbally notified of prohibited work or, by the force of deeply ingrained self-censorship, stay clear of controversial work.

Controversial books may include sociological works that discuss Iran's pre-Islamic past or the secular roots of Iranian society. For example, the recent work of Ahmad Shamlu,[12] a renowned modern poet, has been banned since the publication of its first six volumes in the early years after the revolution. *Ketab-e Koucheh* (Book of the Street) is a compilation of 120 volumes of popular Persian sayings, slang and proverbs. The popular lexicon in Iran has strong secular and anti-clerical elements.

---

[11] They were among fifty Iranian intellectuals in exile who signed a 1992 declaration opposing the *fatwa*; see Chapter 7.

[12] In 1991, Ahmad Shamlu was one of twenty-two writers from sixteen countries to receive the Lillian Hellman and Dashiell Hammett Award for persecuted writers from the Fund for Free Expression. The Fund is a division of Human Rights Watch.

The work of persons in exile can also be controversial, especially those persons who actively oppose the policies of the government abroad. Even the mention of their names or use of their portraits can be problematic. Two examples:

•The book *Sad Film Dar Tarikh Cinema-y Iran* (A Hundred Films in the History of Cinema in Iran) by Ahmed Amini was originally published with a picture of Parviz Sayad[13] as the popular character Samad on the cover along with many other photographs. After publication, it was gathered up and banned. A new version was published with a plain colored cover.

•The book *Sher No As Agaz Ta Emrooz* (Modern Poetry from the Beginning to the Present), compiled by Mohammad Hoghoogi, initially included poems by the modern poet Nader Naderpour and was banned in November 1992. A new version was published without Naderpour's poems.

Censorship and control are a part of the everyday life of most writers and publishers. Despite the absence of official orders, the government's role in institutionalizing control and censorship is unmistakable -- even when they occur at the hands of the apparently freewheeling market forces or at the behest of pressure groups speaking for the "public." For some writers and publishers, however, government-imposed sanctions extend beyond censorship to confiscation of property, prosecution and imprisonment.

The following section first sets out the government procedures governing the censorship and publication of books and analyses the unique role played by publishers in effectuating government censorship and the risks they face. The section concludes with the profiles of three writers, Ali-Akbar Saidi-Sirjani, Moniroo Ravanipoor and Shahrnoush Parsipour, whose books have been banned by the government.

---

[13] Parviz Sayad is a playwright and film director whose work in exile has been critical of the Islamic Republic of Iran. For example, his play *Mohakemeh-ye Cinema Rex* (The Cinema Rex Trial) suggests that Islamic partisans who now form part of the current Iranian government were responsible for the deaths of several hundred persons during the burning of the Rex movie theater in Abadan during the revolution.

The Censorship Process

Regulations issued by the Ministry of Culture and Islamic Guidance govern the publication and release of books (see Chapter 1). The Ministry requires that an approval permit be issued at two stages of the publication process before a book's final release. The two stages of approval occur at a time when any required amendment will result in significant additional costs for the author, publisher, printer and binder, and a ban will lead to irrecoverable loss. Official permits, however, do not guarantee the long-term circulation of a book or provide protection for the writer or publisher against prosecution or mob violence.

The direct involvement of the Ministry in the process of publication commences when a book is at an advanced stage. In a deceptively liberal gesture, the Ministry does not require pre-approval of manuscripts for publication. Instead, a publisher is free to select manuscripts for publication and forward them to the printer. The printer typesets the manuscript and prints copies at the expense of the publisher or author. The printer then binds one copy of the printed book, gives it a temporary blank cover and submits it along with a form indicating name of author and publisher, number of copies printed and date of publication for consideration by the Ministry's Censorship Committee.[14]

The committee responds to the request in one of three ways. If it approves the book, an official permit is granted to release the book from the printer to the binder for binding and covering. The name of the binder is specified in the permit. The publisher or author naturally incurs the costs of these processes.

Alternatively, however, if the committee disapproves of portions of the book, the Ministry will call upon either the publisher or the author and will notify him or her verbally of the faulty portions, with instructions to make the necessary changes and resubmit the book for consideration. As discussed elsewhere in this report, the relevant officials -- in this case, the members of the Ministry's Censorship Committee --

---

[14] Due to the significant effort and cost associated with the printing of a single copy of a book, limited print runs are not economical.

leave no written record of their "suggested amendments."[15] Modification at this stage is very costly; it involves changing the entire signature of pages (usually a 16-page unit or grouping of pages) where an alteration must occur, in every printed copy of the book. The burden of these costs once again falls on the publisher or author.

As a third option, the committee instead of issuing an official order banning a book may merely not respond to the request for releasing galleys to the binder. In practice, no time limits exist for the committee's consideration of submitted works, which has lasted from days to years. Pending a government response, the books are stored at the printer's facilities until such time as, due to financial and space constraints, the printer will either burn the books or recycle them. In some cases, a representative of the Ministry personally supervises this process.

However, if a permit is granted for the bindery, ten copies of the first print and five copies of subsequent prints of the book are given to the Ministry for the second approval and pricing. At this second stage of review, the Ministry can either price the book and issue a permit allowing for its distribution and sale; require modifications; or merely choose not to respond to the pending request. Where the Ministry fails to respond for a prolonged period of time, the printer, once again under financial and space constraints, destroys the books.

Pricing is used as a tool of censorship in one of two ways. A book is either priced so high that no one can afford it, or so low that the cost of production, especially the purchase of black market paper, cannot be

---

[15] Esmail Fassih, an Iranian author, in describing the interaction of a fictional author with the Ministry, writes that he is "urged to rephrase or omit or think about certain passages, sentences or words that may contain ambiguous remarks or conflict with the Islamic Republic." He continues to describe the long-anticipated approval of the Ministry:

> The okay, incidentally, will be an oral one. There won't be any official permit. Nothing on paper. Nobody is censoring anybody to give a permit. Go ahead and print it in n-thousand copies and then bring in five copies for price setting and the final authorization for distribution. Heh, heh. Go ahead.

Esmail Fassih, "The Status: A Day in the Life of a Contemporary Iranian Writer," *Third World Quarterly*, Vol. 9, No. 3, July 1987, pp. 825 and 836.

recovered. Publishers who produce official publications, however, have access to government-subsidized paper, and as a matter of course the price of their publications exceeds cost.

Controlling the availability of paper also is an effective means of controlling writers. The distribution and sale of paper have been the exclusive prerogative of the Ministry. Paper is a scarce and rationed import, particularly since the destruction of Iranian paper plants during the Iran-Iraq war. The Ministry allocates paper only for approved purposes to selected persons or entities. All others must buy paper in the "free" or black market at considerably higher prices. Despite the nature of or stage at which "modifications" are requested, a book that is ultimately released must be printed uniformly and without variations of paper, which can add a crippling cost: paper purchased on the "free," black market is particularly risky, because there is no guarantee that the same color and texture of paper as in the original can be found to implement the changes without having to reprint the entire work.

This long and uncertain process must be repeated with every renewed edition or print run of the book. It is not uncommon for books that have been approved for the first, second or third printings to be blocked at a subsequent attempt. Nor is it uncommon for books with official permits to be banned within weeks of their release.

Even after passing all the cumbersome stages of government approval and control, books are then subject to the "public" test of propriety, which in fact constitutes the final stage of censorship. While ostensibly expressing the free exchange of ideas, these voices echo the more extreme, erratic and uncompromising factions within the government itself, or are associated with the clerical regime, and often translate into a government ban of previously approved books. The primary champion of these "public" attacks is the government-owned or government-affiliated press, each newspaper and magazine invested with its own political alliance.[16]

---

[16] The various tendencies that control newspapers are described in Chapter 2.

PUBLISHERS AND CENSORSHIP

After the revolution, the new government seized the assets of many of the publishing houses in existence under the Shah. A notable example is the government's expropriation of Entesharat Amir Kabir (Amir Kabir Publications), one of the largest publishing houses prior to the revolution, including its seven book shops and print shop. The company's founder and owner, Abdolrahim Jafari, was imprisoned for eleven months.[17] Confiscated property valued in excess of $1 million was then transferred to the Islamic Propaganda Organization, a semi-autonomous foundation.[18]

It is estimated that over seventy percent of the books published in Iran are funded by the government and state-allied foundations.[19] A number of foundations receive government funds and preferential paper allotments and publish books largely in line with the thinking and propaganda needs of the regime.[20] Due to their alliance with influential factions within the government, these entities do not need to fear censorship. Private publishers by contrast, lead a perilous existence and operate under severe financial and government constraints. Not surprisingly, a significant number of independent publishers go out of business.

---

[17] Fassih, "The Status: A Day in the Life of a Contemporary Iranian Writer," p. 833.

[18] *Andeesheh va Paykar*, No. 2, 2nd Supplement, pp. 59-65.

[19] Fassih, "The Status: A Day in the Life of a Contemporary Iranian Writer," pp. 832-833.

[20] Such state-affiliated foundations include the Anjoman Islami Nasherin (Islamic Society of Publishers), Hozeih-e Andisheh va Honar Islami (the Center of Islamic Thoughts and Arts), Sazeman Tabliqat Islami (Islamic Propaganda Organization), Daneshjooyan Mosalman Peyro Khat Imam (Muslim Students Following the Line of the Imam), Bonyad Mostazafin (Foundation of the Dispossessed), Bonyad Andishe Islami (Foundation for Islamic Thought), Bonyad Shaheed (Martyr's Foundation), Sazman Chap va Entesharat Vezarat Ershad Islami (Print and Publishing Organization of the Ministry for Islamic Culture and Guidance) and Kanun Parvaresh-e-Fekri Kudakan va Nojavanan (Center for the Intellectual Development of Children and Young Adults).

As discussed above, the overall process of book publishing encourages private entities, such as the publisher and printer, to assume the role of censor to avoid the often insupportable financial sanctions imposed by government policies. In addition to sanctions, there are at least three other factors that prompt the independent publisher to act as censor and steer clear of even slightly controversial work.

First, publishers are required to renew their permits every six months or every year. Publishers associated with "subversive" work risk non-renewal of their permits. For this reason, the permit of the publishing house Nashr-e Noo was not renewed in 1990. Nashr-e Noo had published the banned publications of Saidi-Sirjani, *Sima-ye Do Zan* (Portrait of Two Women) and *Zahak-e Mardoosh* (Zabak the Snake Man).

Second, publishers associated with controversial work have been victims of mob violence, which is apparently condoned by the authorities. Two examples:

• The publishing house Nashr-e Nogreh was fire-bombed on November 6, 1992 in Tehran. It had previously published Shahrnoush Parsipour's banned book *Zanan Bedoon-e Mardan* (Women without Men). The bomb, which was planted in front of the publishing house, caused a large fire and inflicted significant damage on the facility, causing its temporary closure.[21]

•The publishing house Niloofar in Tehran was bombed by a Molotov cocktail in 1992. Sources in Iran are reluctant to offer specifics, but report that many of the books it had published were banned previous to this incident.

Third, for publication of books deemed "anti-revolutionary" by the government, publishers have been prosecuted along with the writers. For example:

•Mohammad Reza Aslani, owner of the publishing house Nashr-e Nogreh, was imprisoned, tried and acquitted with Shahrnoush Parsipour after publication of her banned book *Zanan Bedoon-e Mardan* (Women without Men) (See below).

---

[21] *Keyhan Hava'i*, November 12, 1992, p. 1.

• According to a source whose account Middle East Watch has not been able to confirm, Sadegh Samie, the owner of the publishing house Astan Sara, was tried with Forough Shahab for publication of her book *Se Hezar or Yek Shab* (Three Thousand and One Nights). The trial was held before the general courts in Tehran in the summer of 1992, and they were acquitted of anti-revolutionary charges.

Under such conditions, finding a publisher can present an unsurmountable problem for many writers. As one author told Middle East Watch, "Some publishers stand by you and some run."

PROFILES OF BANNED WRITERS

Ali-Akbar Saidi-Sirjani

Ali-Akbar Saidi-Sirjani, a writer, essayist and social critic renowned in Iran, has been a particularly outspoken critic of the Islamic Republic's censorship policies during the past four years. Since 1989, there has been a complete ban on seventeen of his books. In keeping with its customary practice, the government has not issued an official banning order. The ban, nevertheless, has been all-encompassing and financially ruinous for him, his family and his publishers.

The government's interaction with Saidi-Sirjani has been nothing short of duplicitous. In 1989, officials of the Ministry of Culture and Islamic Guidance notified him that apart from two of his books they had no objection to his work. The Ministry had not officially banned these two books but merely had not responded to his request for the initial permit required for binding the second printing of *Dar Astin-e Moraqqa'*, pending since 1985, and the first print run of *Ey Kutah Astinan*, pending since 1988.[22] The printed copies of *Dar Astin-e Moraqqa'* were subsequently confiscated and pulped. Saidi-Sirjani, relying on the government's representations, engaged publishers to print numerous copies of his works. But none of his work has been released to this day.

[22] The titles of these books do not lend themselves to simple translation. Both titles draw on verses of poetry from Hafez and play on the themes of hypocrisy and abuse of power by governing authorities.

The ban imposed on his work has been two-pronged. For some books, the Ministry has not issued the initial permit necessary to bind the printed copies, including the first edition, of the six-volume *Tafsir-e Soorabadi* (Exegesis of the Koran by Soorabadi) submitted for approval in 1990; the fifth edition of the two-volume *Tarikh-e Bidari-ye Iranian* (History of the Awakening of Iranians) submitted in 1990; and the third printing of the two-volume *Vaqaye' Ettefaqiyy* (Incidental Occurrences) submitted in 1990. For his other books, the Ministry granted the initial permit necessary for binding, but then did not respond to the numerous requests pending for the second permit required to release the now printed, bound and covered copies. These books include: the fourth edition of *Sima-ye Do Zan* (Portrait of Two Women) submitted in 1989; the fifth edition of *Zahhak-e Mardoosh* (Zahak the Snake Man) submitted in 1989; the first printing of *Bichareh Esfandiyar* (Poor Esfandiar) submitted in 1991; and the first printing of *Tah Basat* (Remaining Stock) submitted in 1990.

The financial burden resulting from the Ministry's ban on of his work has been severe. For example, typesetting the six volumes of *Tafsir-e Soorabadi* cost over 2,000,000 tomans (approximately $11,800). The 15,000 copies of the fifth edition of *Zahak-e Mardoosh* cost 1,200,000 tomans (approximately $7,000) for their jacketing alone.

Some of Saidi-Sirjani's banned work has been particularly popular in Iran. The first four printings of *Zahak-e Mardoosh*, totaling 25,000 copies, sold out in a week. The first three prints of *Sima-ye Do Zan* totaling 20,000 copies, sold out in six months.

Saidi-Sirjani is one of the few people residing in Iran to voice criticism of government policy publicly. In the last four years, he has written nine letters to government officials, including President Rafsanjani, Spiritual Leader Ayatollah Khamenei and members of the parliament, inquiring about the status of his work and objecting to the censorship policies of the government and misapplication of the law. In his customary sarcastic style, addressing President Rafsanjani in a letter dated October 9, 1992, he asks:

> If my writings have faults, why do you not specify them and enlighten me? If however the penalty of my actions, as the cautious writers of *Keyhan* claim, is severe, why do

> you not prosecute and punish me so that I may serve as an example for others?[23]

The government has not responded to any of his letters or acted on the many pending requests for the release of his books. The hard-line newspaper *Keyhan,* however, responded to his letters, initially in December 1992 in its subsidiary *Keyhan-e Hava'i,* which is published and distributed exclusively abroad, and subsequently in its domestic publication. *Keyhan Hava'i* stated that Saidi-Sirjani knows better than anyone else the reasons for which his work has been banned, namely that they are against Islam and moral values. As an example of Saidi-Sirjani's anti-Islamic work, it cites a sentence from his book *Ey Kutah Astinan*: "In Iran, prior to the Arab conquest, there existed a distinct and authentic culture with multiple and diverse facets."[24]

A censored version of the banned *Ey Kutah Astinan* appeared in bookstores sometime in late 1991. Saidi-Sirjani only became aware of this private edition in late summer 1992. He filed a complaint with the General Prosecutor's Office in December 1992 and was granted a hearing that same month. The court has not yet ruled on his complaint, but, soon after the hearing, all copies of the unlawful book disappeared from bookstores.

Saidi-Sirjani has also been subject to constant vilification in the Iranian press as a submissive servant of imperialism, an activist of the Communist Tudeh party, a panegyrist of the Pahlavi regime, and an agent of SAVAK, the Shah's secret police.

Moniroo Ravanipoor

Since the 1979 revolution, Moniroo Ravanipoor has become a popular author celebrated for her unique folkloric style and distinguished by her focus on issues facing women; in an almost parallel progression, she has been the object of increasing vilification by the state-affiliated

---

[23] The letter was published in Persian-language publications abroad, as well as photocopied and circulated hand-to-hand in Iran and faxed abroad. Translation by Middle East Watch.

[24] Quoted in *Keyhan Hava'i,* November 25, 1992. Translation by Middle East Watch.

media. And with her voice no longer confined to restricted circles, the government has subjected her work to increased scrutiny and censorship--including work which had previously met government requirements.

The momentum of criticism and attack in the government-affiliated press started with her very popular collection of short stories, *Sanghay Sheytan* (Devil's Stones). Typical was an attack appearing in *Keyhan* newspaper, titled "Tohin be Shahidan va Fesad Akhlagi" (Insult to Martyrs and Corruption of Mores). *Sanghay Sheytan* had been a great success, with 10,000 copies of its first two printings selling out in a week. A third printing of the book was banned by the Ministry of Culture and Islamic Guidance in 1990.

Following this incident, her book *Kanizoo* was banned at its third printing in December 1991. The Ministry required modification of a number of sections of the book. After twenty months of negotiated modifications, the book entered its third edition in 1993.

Ravanipoor's difficulties with censorship extend beyond these two books, however. In a recent interview with the magazine *Gardoon*, in response to the question "What portion of the work you have produced has not been published?" she stated: "One half of my work."[25] In at least one instance, the publication of her work was affected indirectly by the Ministry of Culture and Islamic Guidance: the appearance of her book *Del Foolad* (Steel Heart) was delayed when the Ministry canceled the operating permit of its publisher, Shirazi.[26]

In the same interview, the author questioned government policies on speech, stating that "the writer is the creator of his or her own work....In my view, no one has the right to give an opinion and then ask that a position [taken by an author] be amended before issuing a publishing permit."[27]

She also alluded to officials' inability to tell realistic fiction from an author's fancy. Recalling a conversation with a Ministry official after she had submitted her manuscript of *Del Foolad* for approval, she stated:

[25] *Gardoon*, July 1993, p. 26. Translations by Middle East Watch.

[26] Ibid.

[27] Ibid.

> [He] told me, "After all, a single woman would never go and live in a house where a [young man] is living." Well, this is being misinformed. When someone in power doesn't know how many thousands of women flee to Tehran -- what can one do? It is not only a question of differences of opinion and taste; lack of awareness and naiveté are also involved.[28]

Noting the strength of tradition in Iran, Ravanipoor concluded the interview commenting on the constraints limiting women artists.

> Breaking tradition is not an easy matter. When you want to break with some of the wrong traditions, you must be able to withstand flogging [public persecution]. I in effect have broken with traditions....A woman in order to exist must break with tradition...You wish to say look I have thoughts, I have things to say, I am a human being, I am not in a harem.[29]

Ravanipoor's latest book, *Siria Siria*, was published in 1993.

Shahrnoush Parsipour

Shahrnoush Parsipour, a novelist of much acclaim, was twice imprisoned for her book *Zanan Bedoun-e Mardan* (Women Without Men), following vehement attacks against the book in the state-affiliated media. All her work, including her earlier best-selling novel *Touba va Ma'nay-e Shab* (Touba and the Meaning of Night), was banned. After a lapse of two years, she was tried and acquitted. But the bombing of her publisher's facilities after the trial, and the continued ban on her work, are grim reminders of the limited protection of judicial processes.

In June 1990, Parsipour published *Zanan Bedoun-e Mardan*, a collection of interconnected short stories written in Tehran and Paris prior to the revolution. The book presents a critical assessment of the role of women in society. It had undergone revisions required by the

[28] Ibid.

[29] Ibid., p. 29.

Ministry of Culture and Islamic Guidance and been granted a permit for publication. Five thousand copies of the book sold out within weeks. A series of attacks ensued in the state-affiliated press, notably in *Bayan* and *Sureh*[30] magazines and *Keyhan* newspaper. In customary fashion, these attacks aimed at the person of the author, at writers, literature and publishers in general, and at the Ministry for allegedly undermining social mores and corrupting values.

In August 1990, Parsipour and her publisher, Mohammad-Reza Aslani from the Nashr Nogreh publishing house, were summoned to the Anti-Vice Department of the Revolutionary Prosecutor's Office for interrogation. They were then imprisoned for five weeks without charge or trial, after which Parsipour was released on bail. Their file was transferred to the General Prosecutor's Office, and trial was set for February 1992.

Two officials of the Ministry responsible for reviewing her book and issuing the permit for publication were set for trial along with Parsipour and Aslani. The charges against Parsipour involved *Zanan Bedoun-e Mardan* and, in addition, her novel *Sagh va Zemestan Boland* (Dog and a Long Winter), which was also printed in June 1990 but had not been granted the permit necessary for its release.

The February 1992 trial date was postponed. In March, Parsipour presented herself to the General Prosecutor's Office and requested that her bail be lifted; she asked that the family property posted as bail for her be released. In return for releasing the property, Parsipour was imprisoned for one month. She reportedly was beaten in prison during this time. Bail was again posted, this time money offered by a friend, and she was released in April.

The trial ultimately took place in the summer of 1992 in the general courts, at a time when Parsipour was outside the country.[31] The

---

[30] *Bayan* was published by the Tehran Combatant Clergy Association (breakaway group) until March 1991, when it was closed by the government (See Chapter 2). *Sureh* is a magazine published by the Islamic Propagation Organization, a semi-autonomous foundation.

[31] As another example of the complexities of government policy, in the spring of 1992 Parsipour was granted permission to leave the country and conduct a year-long tour of North America and Europe.

court acquitted all the parties involved, finding that none of Parsipour's books contained anti-revolutionary material.

Since her 1990 arrest, however, the publication of all her books has been effectively banned, including her 1989 novel *Touba va Ma'nay-e Shab*. The novel had been a national best seller: three printings totaling 22,000 copies sold out in six months.

Although no official order has been issued banning Parsipour's work, publishers are unwilling to assume the risks that publishing the work entails. The Ministry also "advises" publishers against such ventures. In fact, the publication of her fourth work *Agl Aby* (Blue Reason) was indefinitely interrupted in 1990 by the publisher after the events that followed publication of *Zanan Bedoun-e Mardan*. The bombing of *Nashr-e Nogreh* publishing house in November 1992, described above, is a reminder of the uncertainty that surrounds her work even after the trial. At present, no copies of her books appear in bookstores, although pirated photocopies of her work are popular items in the black market at inflated prices.

Parsipour had experienced prosecution before these recent events. She was arrested in the early revolutionary period in 1981, imprisoned until 1986 and released without any official charges brought against her. She also has a history of imprisonment under the Shah: in the spring of 1974, she resigned from her position in state-owned television to protest the execution of the poet and journalist Khosrow Golesorkhi and his colleague Keramatollah Daneshian. She was arrested in the fall of that year and imprisoned for a period of fifty-four days, then released without being charged or tried for any offence.

7
THE *FATWA* AGAINST SALMAN RUSHDIE AND ITS EXTENSION TO IRANIANS

I inform the proud Muslim people of the world that the author of The Satanic Verses book which is against Islam, the Prophet and the Koran, and all involved in its publication who were aware of its content, are sentenced to death. . . . [Anyone who dies in the cause of ridding the world of Salman Rushdie] will be regarded as a martyr and go directly to heaven.

-- *Ayatollah Khomeini*
February 14, 1989
on Tehran Radio[1]

With Ayatollah Khomeini's religious edict (*fatwa* in Arabic), the battle over freedom of expression crossed the Iranian border to threaten the citizen of another country and, by extension, anyone involved with his novel. The edict infringes on free expression under Article 19 of the International Covenant on Civil and Political Rights, to which Iran is a signatory. Article 19 protects "the freedom to impart information and ideas of all kinds, regardless of frontiers" and to do so "in writing" and "in the form of art." The covenant protects even expression that deeply offends or angers, as in the case of *The Satanic Verses*.

It has been argued by some that the *fatwa* was an individual pronouncement, and thus protected speech itself.[2] But no government or individual has a protected right under Article 19 or Article 20

---

[1] Quoted in Article 19, *Fiction, Fact and the Fatwa: A Chronology of Censorship--Revised* (October 1992), p. 1.

[2] By way of example, on February 19, 1992, Ayatollah Mohammad Imami-Kashani, a member of the Supreme Council of Guardians, stated in his Friday sermon: "How is it that a corrupt man is free to blaspheme and to offend that which is holy to a billion Muslims, but a holy man is not free to ask that the command of God be executed?" (*Iran Times*, February 26, 1993, p. 1.) In a meeting with Middle East Watch, on February 13, 1993, Deputy Foreign Minister Javad Zarif took the same line, wanting to know if Ayatollah Khomeini's statement should not be considered free speech.

(concerning incitement to violence) to issue a death threat aimed at *specific* individuals.[3]

Ayatollah Khomeini's religious edict was born of peculiarly political circumstances. The *fatwa* came only after the book was banned in India, South Africa, Bangladesh, Sudan, Sri Lanka and Pakistan, and after violent protests against the book had erupted in India, Pakistan and Britain. It significantly followed a cease-fire that ended the eight-year Iran-Iraq war, at a time when calls for moderation by the then-Speaker of the Parliament Ali-Akbar Hashemi-Rafsanjani, President Ali Khamenei and successor-designate as Supreme Religious Leader, Ayatollah Hossein Ali Montazeri,[4] were gaining ground. It is telling that Rushdie has been accused not only of apostasy but also of advancing the "Western plot" against Islam and the underdeveloped world, a central theme of the more radical factions in Iran. The debate over who was more revolutionary and who more Islamic gained renewed vitality with Ayatollah Khomeini's *fatwa*, a process that favored the radical factions.

For several years after the *fatwa* was issued, Western governments remained largely silent or selectively vocal, using the *fatwa* as a

---

[3] The Human Rights Watch policy statement on "hate speech" reads, in relevant part:

> Any restriction on the content of expression must be based on direct and immediate incitement of acts of violence, discrimination or hostility against an individual or clearly defined group of persons in circumstances in which such violence, discrimination or hostility is imminent and alternative measures to prevent such conduct are not reasonably available. For this purpose, "violence" refers to physical attack; "discrimination" refers to the actual deprivation of a benefit to which similarly situated people are entitled or the imposition of a penalty or sanction not imposed on other similarly situated people; and "hostility" refers to criminal intimidation.

That is, even the most protective definition of provocative speech cannot, in our view, include protection for the death threat issued against Salman Rushdie.

[4] Ayatollah Montazeri's refusal to endorse the *fatwa* contributed to his being dropped by Ayatollah Khomeini as his designated successor. See also Chapter 9.

bargaining chip in their relations with Iran.[5] Recently, however, due to persistent pressure from human rights and international freedom of expression organizations, a number of Western countries, including Britain, the United States, Canada, Belgium and the Nordic countries, have adopted official positions condemning the *fatwa*. Notable instances include the official statements issued by the British and the U.S. governments. On February 2, 1993, U.K. Foreign Minister Douglas Hurd stated that Iran's failure to repudiate the *fatwa* and the bounty "inevitably prevents the establishment of full and friendly relations between Britain and Iran."[6] On February 11, U.S. President Clinton's then-Communications Secretary, George Stephanopoulos, stated:

> We unequivocally condemn the *fatwa*. We do not believe this is a private matter between Mr. Rushdie and Iran. We do not believe that people should be killed for writing books. We regard the *fatwa* as a violation of Mr. Rushdie's basic human rights, and therefore as a violation of international law.[7]

On July 9, 1993 at the Tokyo summit meeting of the Members of the Group of Seven, the U.S. and U.K. once again voiced their concerns over the *fatwa*. In their Political Declaration, the Group of Seven stated, "Concerned about aspects of Iran's behavior, we call upon its government to participate constructively in international efforts for peace and stability and to cease actions contrary to these objectives."

The United Nations has also made headway on the issue of the *fatwa*. On March 10, 1993 the United Nations Human Rights Commission adopted a strongly-worded resolution condemning Iran's abuse of human rights, with special reference to the right of freedom of

---

[5] On the shifting diplomatic stances of the European countries with Iran in relation to the *fatwa*, see American Association of Publishers and the Fund for Free Expression (a division of Human Rights Watch), *Threat Against Salman Rushdie* (New York: 1992).

[6] Article 19, *Events Immediately Preceding and Subsequent to Council of Ministers Edinburgh Summit Conclusion* (London: June 1993), p. 2.

[7] Ibid., p. 3.

expression, and decided to extend the mandate of the special representative for a further year.[8] The Commission reaffirmed that "[g]overnments are accountable for assassinations and attacks by their agents against persons on the territory of another State, as well as for the incitement, approval or wilful condoning of such act."[9] In specific reference to Salman Rushdie, the Commission expressed its grave concern that "there are continuing threats to the life of a citizen of another State which have the support of the Government of the Islamic Republic of Iran and whose case is mentioned in the report of the Special Representative."[10]

The regime in Tehran, for its part, has issued contradictory and ambiguous pronouncements on the significance and implications of the *fatwa*. In February 1989, then-President Ali Khamenei suggested that if Salman Rushdie "repents" and apologizes to Muslims, "it is possible that the people may pardon him."[11] Khamenei was admonished, and Rushdie's apology rejected, by Ayatollah Khomeini. In February 1990, President Rafsanjani attempted to diminish the importance of, and distance the government from, the *fatwa* by stating that it was merely "an opinion of a religious jurisprudence expert."[12] The day after this statement, the Head of the Judiciary, Ayatollah Mohammad Yazdi, with the confirmation of Ayatollah Ali Khamenei, now the Supreme Religious Leader, stated: "Through a legal and judicial eye we announce explicitly that this verdict is a binding and irrevocable one and not a religious judgment alone."[13] Recently, in an attempt once again to distance the Iranian government from the death threat, Ali-Akbar Nateq Nuri, the

---

[8] *Report on the Situation of Human Rights in the Islamic Republic of Iran by the Commission on Human Rights* (U.N. Doc. E/CN.4/1993/L.35), March 4, 1993. The resolution was passed by twenty-three votes to eleven, with fourteen abstentions.

[9] Ibid., p. 2.

[10] Ibid., p. 5.

[11] Article 19, *Fiction, Fact and the Fatwa*, p. 3.

[12] London *Keyhan*, February 22, 1990, as reported in FBIS, March 15, 1990.

[13] Ibid.

speaker of the Iranian parliament, stated: "We have not and will not send out mercenaries to kill the infidel [Salman Rushdie], since this is not our policy."[14] Several government officials have also attempted to draw a distinction between the government and the Fifteenth of Khordad Foundation, declaring it to be an independent organization over which they did not have control.

In reality, it is not possible to draw a line of separation between the Iranian government and Ayatollah Khomeini's *fatwa*. In a system of governance based on *velayat-e faqih*, there is no authority superior to that of the supreme religious leader. Since February 1989, the *fatwa* has been reaffirmed by the new Supreme Religious Leader Ayatollah Ali Khamenei, President Rafsanjani, Head of the Judiciary Ayatollah Yazdi, and members of the parliament. On February 17, 1993, for example, two-thirds of the Majlis, endorsed the death sentence against Rushdie. The $1 million reward offered on February 15, 1989 by Hojatoleslam Hassan Sane'i, an influential Iranian cleric at the head of the semi-autonomous Fifteenth of Khordad Foundation and former aide to Ayatollah Khomeini, to anyone who kills Salman Rushdie has been twice increased -- in March 1991 to $2 million, and in February 1993 by an unspecified amount. In sum, the Iranian government is responsible for the *fatwa*.

VIOLENT CONSEQUENCES

Ayatollah Khomeini's death threat has had real and tragic implications for the persons targeted. Since the issuance of the *fatwa*, Rushdie has been forced to go into hiding and live under police protection. Hitoshi Igarashi, the Japanese translator of *The Satanic Verses*, was stabbed to death in July 1991 by an unknown assailant who evaded capture. In the same month, Ettore Capriolo, the Italian translator of the book, was stabbed and injured, and also has been forced to live under police protection. Around the world, numerous bookstores carrying the book have been bombed and its publishers threatened.

The most recent target of the *fatwa* is Aziz Nesin, an internationally-known Turkish humorist and chairman of The Writers' Union of Turkey. On February 3, 1993, Nesin announced that he was

---

[14] *Iran Times*, May 7, 1993, p. 1.

going to have *The Satanic Verses* translated and published in Turkey. The novel has been banned in Turkey since 1989. On February 4, an article in the Iranian daily *Jomhouri-ye Islami,* affiliated with the Supreme Religious Leader Ayatollah Khamenei, extended the *fatwa* to Nesin and stated: "He no longer has a place among Muslims and should like Rushdie, be killed."[15] Hojatoleslam Hassan Sane'i urged Nesin to reconsider his decision in light of the death sentence on Rushdie, or else bear the consequences of his action.[16] Most recently, on July 15, 1993, the Ministry of Culture and Islamic Guidance banned all Nesin's works in Iran and ordered removal of his books from bookstores.[17]

The Iranian government often justifies the *fatwa* by referring to the death and injury of numerous Muslims in India and Pakistan in protesting *The Satanic Verses.*[18] In no instance, however, can a death threat be justified. Furthermore, neither the author nor *The Satanic Verses* is the cause of these deaths or injuries; they resulted from clashes with security forces.[19] Article 19, in fact, protects Salman Rushdie's right to expression just as much as it protects all persons' right to peaceful protest. Similarly, all violations of the right to peaceful protest must be uniformly condemned.

Many have spoken against the *fatwa*. But the uniquely severe reaction of the Iranian government to the declaration of a group of exiled Iranian intellectuals, artists and professionals against the *fatwa* and its immediate implications for these individuals (see below) are a reminder of the common threads that bind Salman Rushdie's fate to that

---

[15] *Info-Turk* (Belgium), February 1993, p. 7.

[16] *Turkish Probe* (Turkey), February 23, 1993, p. 17.

[17] *Iran Times*, July 23, 1993, p. 2.

[18] The Iranian government routinely refers to the Muslims who lost their lives in these demonstrations as martyrs and commemorates the anniversary of their death.

[19] The circumstances surrounding the death and injury of the individuals protesting in India and Pakistan is beyond the scope of this report. International standards, however, place strict limits on the use of force by law-enforcement officials, which may have been exceeded in these cases.

of Iranians inside and outside Iran. They are all victims of the same brand of intolerance. The Rushdie affair also highlights the lack of centralized authority and uncertainty that plagues the day-to-day existence of the Iranian intellectual and artistic community.

Declaration of Iranians in Exile Condemning the *Fatwa*

On the third anniversary of Ayatollah Khomeini's *fatwa* against Salman Rushdie *et. al.*, in March 1992, a group of fifty Iranians in exile condemned the *fatwa*. Calling the religious edict "inhuman" and freedom of speech "one of the most precious achievements of mankind," the declaration adds: "[A]s Voltaire remarked, this freedom would be meaningless unless individuals had the right to blaspheme." It also takes note of "the merciless pressure of religious censorship" that exists inside Iran.[20] This was the first time that Iranians collectively had lent their names to a condemnation of the *fatwa* as an abrogation of the right to freedom of expression.

The signatories have since been subjected to intense vilification in the Iranian press for being instruments of Western culture and interests, enemies of Islam and the Islamic Revolution, monarchists and imperialist lackeys. The work of fifty original signatories has been effectively banned in Iran by pronouncement of a senior cleric, and the terms of the original *fatwa* extended to them by the official news organ of Supreme Religious Leader Ayatollah Khamenei.

The vilification campaign against the fifty signatories was led by the government-owned newspapers *Keyhan* and *Keyhan Hava'i*, the daily *Jomhouri-ye Islami*, affiliated with Supreme Religious Leader Ayatollah Khamenei, and the daily *Salam*, published by the Tehran Combatant Clergy Association (breakaway group). As is customary, in the process, government authorities were accused of inaction, until factional pressure culminated in a rare written order from the Ministry of Culture and Islamic Guidance banning the works of two of the signatories. This was the sequence of events:

[20] See Appendix B for full text of the declaration and the names of all signatories as of March 1993.

•On April 15, 1992, *Keyhan Hava'i* stated: "It appears that the Ministry of Culture and Islamic Guidance must in an official manner prevent the publication in the domestic press of the works of these individuals because of their support for Salman Rushdie; in view of the existing laws, this is a request that is both possible and legal."

•On May 8, 1992, Ayatollah Ahmad Jannati, a member of the Council of Guardians, announced in his Friday sermon that the work of all fifty signatories was banned in Iran.

•On May 27, 1992, *Jomhouri-ye Islami,* the news organ associated with Supreme Religious Leader Ayatollah Khamenei, published the names of the signatories and portions of the declaration. It further stated that Ayatollah Khomeini's *fatwa* henceforth would apply to the group of exiled Iranians, by virtue of their support for Salman Rushdie, as well as all who publish their works.

•An editorial in the June 1992 issue of *Keyhan,* after alluding to the Western backing and support afforded Rushdie but not to the Iranians who signed the declaration, asked the signatories rhetorically: "In this case, would it not have been better if you would not have been so foolish and at least would not have put your own lives in danger?"

•In November 1992, the Ministry of Culture and Islamic Guidance issued a rare written order banning specifically the work of two of the signatories to the declaration: poets Nader Naderpour[21] and Esmail Khoei. The order cited their support of Salman Rushdie as reason for the ban and relied on Article 6(9) of the Press Law.[22]

---

[21] In 1993, Nader Naderpour was one of twenty-six writers from fifteen countries to receive the Lillian Hellman and Dashiell Hammett Award for persecuted writers from the Fund for Free Expression. The Fund is a division of Human Rights Watch.

[22] Article 6(9) of the Press Law provides:

> Publications and the press are free except in the instances where the meaning and principles of Islam and the rights of the public are damaged, as identified in this chapter:

Despite these measures, for the fourth anniversary of the *fatwa*, on February 17, 1993, the number of Iranians in exile signing the declaration increased to 162. In March, the Islamic Revolutionary Prosecutor's Office notified all publishers in Iran that serious consequences would follow from publishing the work of any of the writers now signatories to the declaration. This amounts to a ban on the works of all of them. These people's courage deserves international recognition and support.

... (9) Literary plagiarism as well as narration of material from the press, associations and misguided groups (domestic and foreign) that are against Islam in a manner that propagates them.

8
FILM

In the past decade, despite a significant degree of official control and censorship, Iranian films and directors have been prominently featured at international film festivals and celebrated for their sophisticated style and humanistic portrayals. This decade has also witnessed the emergence of the first generation of female professional film producers -- six in all -- in the industry's sixty-year history. The stories lost in the midst of such achievements, however, are those of refused scripts, storerooms of banned films and censorship. Also lost is the plight of film directors, casts and crews who continue to work and produce in spite of such constraints.

During the first five years after the revolution, the Iranian film industry ground to a halt. Through the revolutionary period, films and movie theaters were targeted as being the embodiment of corrupt Western values. A number of cinemas were destroyed throughout Iran, most notably the Rex Cinema of Abadan, which was burned down in September 1978 at a cost of over 400 lives. However, in a country nearly fifty percent illiterate, officials soon recognized the propaganda potential of film. Despite the Koran's ban on images, the much-quoted edict by Ayatollah Khomeini, "We are not against cinema, we are against prostitution,"[1] signaled a new official policy on film, however ambiguous its mandate.

In 1983, the Farabi Cinema Foundation, a semi-autonomous entity, was created with the assistance of the government. The successes of the Iranian film industry are, in part, due to the persistent efforts of Farabi to enter the international market; the government has given it exclusive control over the import and export of film. Farabi provides assistance to filmmakers through loans, subsidies, studio facilities and "advice" in passing the various stages of censorship. Recognition of Iranian films at international festivals has created a false -- and for the government, convenient -- impression about the apparently broad limits of freedom in Iran, and to this extent has provided little benefit to the film directors, actors and actresses whose travails in making the films are too often unacknowledged.

---

[1] Reza Allamehzadeh, "Islamic Visions and Grand Illusions," *Index on Censorship*, March 1991, p. 13.

In addition to Farabi, a number of other semi-autonomous foundations are also significant players in the film industry. Foremost is Bonyad Mostazafin (Foundation of the Dispossessed), one of the largest and most conservative. Kanun Parvaresh-e Fekri Kudakan va Nojavanan (Center for the Intellectual Development of Children and Young Adults) and Hozeih Honari Sazman Tabligath Islami (Art Center for the Islamic Propagation Organization) are also noteworthy participants in the film industry.

In the past few years, approximately sixty films have been produced annually.[2] It is estimated that sixty to seventy percent of films produced are government-made, either directly or through the network of semi-autonomous foundations. A significant portion of films produced are propaganda vehicles that call young men to the war front, extol the virtues of the Islamic dress code for women and promote the revolution and Islamic government.

Films have much greater popularity than the print media in Iran: it is estimated that annual cinema admission is seventy-five million in a country of some sixty million people.[3] In fact, in response to the acute shortage of movie houses, the Minister of Islamic Culture and Islamic Guidance Ali Larijani announced on March 13, 1993 that, after the Iranian New Year in March, mosques could apply for permits to show films.[4] The government hopes to temper the public's interest in uncontrollable videos and satellite communications by increasing access to the more controllable medium of movie theaters (see also Chapter 5 on satellites). In December 1992, Supreme Religious Leader Ayatollah Khamenei encouraged the production of Islamic films and stated:

> The enemy carries out its cultural onslaught against the Islamic Republic of Iran in an organized way. If our response is not organized, the danger of the enemy's onslaught increases. Therefore, this issue must be addressed seriously and all the competent bodies must

---

[2] Young, "Iranian Cinema Now," p. 27.

[3] Ibid., p. 29.

[4] Reuters, March 14, 1993.

> cooperate and use various methods to neutralize the cultural onslaught of the enemy.[5]

Mosques and films thus have become allies in a crusade to propagate Islam.

Video cassette recorders (VCRs) are regarded by the government as crucial instruments of the foreign cultural onslaught and, for this reason, are illegal. Nonetheless, one report in 1993 estimated the number of VCRs in Iran at 2,500,000 as compared to 5,250,000 television sets.[6] Unable to counter the spread of videos in the black market, the government is apparently reviewing its policy and may move toward legalizing videos. In his March 13 announcement, Culture Minister Larijani stated that the sale, rental or copying of videotapes required a license from the Ministry's film review committee, thereby suggesting that videos may become legal.[7] Yet, on May 30, 1993, in a contradictory statement, the Head of the Judiciary Ayatollah Yazdi announced that "distributors of decadent videos and indecent clothing, offensive to the public"[8] will be given the death sentence.

Foreign films once again have found their way to Iran. *Driving Miss Daisy* and *Dances with Wolves* are examples of Western films shown in the past year, while a large portion of foreign films are from Japan, China and Eastern European countries. Censorship standards applied to foreign films are necessarily less stringent. Women, for example, are shown without the Islamic head cover. Where possible, however, "inappropriate" scenes are cut.

The Iranian government has been particularly sensitive to foreign films that depict Iran in an "unfavorable" light, and it exerts pressure where it can to ban their showing abroad. Two examples:

---

[5] IRIB Television First Program Network, December 10, 1992, as reported in FBIS, December 11, 1992.

[6] Young, "Iranian Cinema Now," p. 27.

[7] *Iran Times*, March 19, 1993, p. 1.

[8] *Iran Times*, June 4, 1993, p. 15.

•In early June 1990, parts of *Naked Gun*, a film made in the United States which alluded to Ayatollah Khomeini, were censored in Turkey due to the Turkish government's concern about damaging relations with Iran.[9] After an official protest by the Iranian government, police barred showings of the film in theaters in Ankara and Istanbul. Theater owners were warned by police that their cinemas would be closed down if they continued to feature the film because then-President Ozal did not wish it to be shown.[10] At the end of June, the company distributing *Naked Gun* announced it would withdraw the film because "No other work received so much pressure. For us no film is worth risking your life."[11] On July 30, 1990, the film was officially banned by the Turkish government.[12]

•In January 1992, the broadcast of the film *Veiled Threat* on Turkish Radio Television led the Iranian government and press to criticize the Turkish government harshly. *Veiled Threat*, directed by Cyrus Nowrasteh, an American of Iranian origin, is about a CIA agent attempting to help an Iranian family escape from the country after the revolution. The Turkish ambassador to Iran was summoned by the Foreign Ministry to hear the strong protests of the Iranian government a week after the showing of the film.[13]

The following section first sets out the government procedures that govern the censorship and production of film. It then assesses the range of restricted topics and the misleading impression left by Iranians' participation in international film festivals, with reference to specific censored films. The section concludes with profiles of two film directors, Bahram Beizai and Mohsen Makhmalbaf, whose films have been banned and censored by the government.

---

[9] This paragraph is drawn from Hensinki Watch, *Freedom of Expression in Turkey: Abuses Continue* (New York: Human Rights Watch, 1991), p. 21.

[10] *Cumhuriyet* (Turkey), June 20, 1990.

[11] *Gunes* (Turkey), June 30, 1990.

[12] *Index on Censorship*, October 1990.

[13] *Milliyet* (Turkey), January 30, 1992.

THE CENSORSHIP PROCESS[14]

Regulations issued by the Ministry of Culture and Islamic Guidance govern the various stages of film production (see Chapter 1). Film production involves four separate stages of censorship and control by the Ministry of Culture and Islamic Guidance. The permits obtained after passing these tortuous stages, however, provide no guarantee or protection to the film, its director, cast or crew.

In the first instance, a film director is required to submit a short sketch, as an outline, to the Ministry's Council of Screenplay Inspection for approval. Once the sketch has been approved, the director is required to submit a working version of the screenplay to the Council for Issuing Production Permit for a subsequent approval.

In the second stage, the film producer must submit a complete list of the proposed members of the cast and crew. Many of the directors, scriptwriters, actors and actresses associated with the previous regime or otherwise out of favor have been denied work permits. Even once approved, the cast and crew are supervised closely by representatives of the Ministry present at the production site.

In the third stage, the completed film is submitted for review and approval to the Ministry's Council of Film Reviewing. The reviewing council has the authority to accept, reject or require modification of the film. While filmmakers may seek a review of the council's determination by the Ministry's High Council of Deputies, they run the risk of another adverse ruling which is final. As a result, they often opt to negotiate with the lower reviewing council. The modifications requested by the Council of Film Reviewing are not given in writing--and, instead, are dictated to the directors. As is customary, required modifications are framed as "suggestions" by the Ministry.

In the final stage, the Ministry accords one of four grades (A, B, C or D) to the film. This grading is based largely on an assessment of what is aesthetically valid and ideologically correct rather than on any objective quality standard. The grade determines access to media for promotion purposes, quality of exposure (e.g. type of theater) and ticket

---

14 This section draws on Houshang Golmakani, "New Times, Same Problems," *Index on Censorship*, March 1992, p. 19; and Allamehzadeh, "Islamic Visions and Grand Illusions," p. 13.

price. Grade A films are screened at the best cinemas in major cities for at least two weeks; the price of the ticket is relatively high, and state radio and television promote the film. Grade D films are confined to smaller cities, prohibited from advertising, and charge cheaper admission, thus obviously generating less return for their creators.

Since 1989, the Ministry no longer requires script approval for a select group of film directors, those whose last film was given an A rating. This does not mean lesser control over the final product, however, for censorship can -- and does -- occur at later stages, when its effects are more expensive for the filmmaker. Film directors whose last film was given a B rating are still required to submit their screenplays but not their sketches for approval; and, finally, film directors whose last film was given a C or D rating are required to secure approval for both outline and screenplay.

The ultimate test of the fate of a film and its director is the "public's" reaction after its screening. Even after securing final official approval, the film may be blocked at a later time, especially in response to criticism from the government-affiliated press.

CENSORED FILMS

The regulations governing evaluation and approval of film content -- set out in Chapter 1 -- have had a far-reaching impact on work dealing with contemporary and social issues. The following films serve as examples:

• Amir Naderi's *Jostejouy Yek* (Search One) was banned from 1980 to 1991. In 1991, it was shown on Iranian state-controlled television after the time-line of the events was dated to the pre-revolutionary period, although its content clearly portrayed a landmark of the revolution, from September 1978, known as Black Friday.[15]

• Barbod Taheri's *Soqut-e'57* (Fall of '57), a documentary film about the revolution, was banned in 1984; its renewed screening was made

[15] This technique is not new to censorship of film in Iran. Dariush Mehrjui's 1968 film *Gav* (Cow) was banned for a year and was released only when the events in the film were re-dated to place them forty years earlier.

contingent on removing footage that showed broad participation in the revolution by secular and leftist groups, armed forces attacks on demonstrators, and even Ayatollah Khomeini's first speech delivered in Tehran's cemetery, in which he condemned the Shah for making cemeteries prosperous.[16]

•Masud Kimiai's *Khateh Ghermez* (Red Line) was made in 1980 and has been banned since its first and only screening at the First Fajr Festival in February 1983. The film portrays the marriage of a former SAVAK agent and a medical student at the time of the revolution. Although it was once amended according to the instructions of the censorship board, it continued to be banned because it linked the origins of the revolution to secular intellectual movements and not only to religious ones.

•Dariush Mehrjui's *Madrese-ye Ke Merafteem* (The School We Used to Go To) was banned from 1980 to 1989, apparently because the time period of the film was uncertain.[17] This, despite the fact that one scene in the film focuses on a newspaper clipping that is dated back to the Shah's regime. It was screened for the first time at the Seventh Fajr Film Festival in 1989, only after it was modified.

•Mehrjui's *Banu* has been banned since its completion in 1991. The film tells the story of a woman who helps and takes into her home a number of deprived persons, only to have them later turn on her and try to evict her from her house. The film was perceived by the government to have contemporary political connotations.

The regulations are invoked on a wide range of topics. But the Iran-Iraq war holds a unique place. While propaganda films about the war abound, critical assessments of the war generally are not tolerated. The following films were banned for being anti-war:

---

[16] Hamid Naficy, "The Development of Islamic Cinema in Iran," *Third World Affairs* (1987), p. 461.

[17] Reza Allamehzadeh, *Sarab Cinemay Eslami Iran* (Mirage of Islamic Cinema in Iran) (1991), pp. 164-165.

•Naderi's *Jostejouy Dow* (Search Two) has been banned since 1981; it deals with the soldiers missing in action in the Iran-Iraq war.

•Bahram Beizai's *Bashu, Garibeh-ye Kuchak* (Bashu the Little Stranger) was banned from 1986 to 1989. The film follows the trail of a child orphaned by the war who makes his way from the south to the north where he finds refuge as a result of a village woman's singular and determined struggles to protect him.

Discussion of Iran's pre-Islamic history and conversion to Islam also are not encouraged. One of the reasons for banning Bahram Beizai's *Margh Yazdegerd* (Death of Yazdegerd) since its completion in 1981 was its particularly sensitive subject matter. It pertains to the death of the last Persian king before the Arab conquest and conversion of Iran to Islam in the seventh century.[18]

The restrictions also have led to significant distortions in the presentation of women on the one hand, and love relationships and family life on the other. Women are required to comply fully with the Islamic dress codes which include covering all hair and wearing clothing that obscures all body curves. Singing or dancing by women is strictly prohibited. Eye or body contact between the sexes is not encouraged. A woman's role is preferably a virtuous and family-oriented one. Thus, the portrayal of intimate relationships presents a real challenge to film directors. In Raksan Bani-Etemad's *Nargess,* in order to communicate the love of a newlywed couple, the camera could not enter their bedroom but instead focused on two pairs of shoes lined up next to each other at the door. In Bani-Etemad's *Kharej as Mahdudeh* (Off Limits), the leading female protagonist is shown in bed fully dressed and alone, although married. Among the criticisms leveled at Mohsen Makhmalbaf's banned film *Nobat-e Asheghi* (Time for Love) was that it depicted human love.

Although in the past couple of years there has been a relative relaxation on the stereotypical happy ending, it still remains a persistent feature of Iranian films. Unhappy endings are condemned for having negative repercussions and undermining the revolutionary spirit. Mehrjui's *Hamoon* and *Ejareh Neshinan* (Tenants), Ali Jakan's *Madiyan* (Mare), Rahman Rezai's *Madar Basteh* (Closed Circuit), and Kimiai's

[18] Judith Miller, "Movies of Iran Struggle for Acceptance," *The New York Times,* July 19, 1992, p. 9.

Goruhban (Sergeant) are examples of films whose endings needed to be modified before they could be screened. Such modifications necessarily result in distortion of the story line.

Despite these impediments, an increasing number of socially critical and insightful films has been produced and screened, for example: Makhmalbaf's *Arousi-e Khouban* (Marriage of the Blessed), Mehrjui's *Hamoon*, and Majid Majidi's *Badook*. The use of music and traditional dances by men has also gained currency.

International Film Festivals and Censored Films

February 1993 marked the eleventh anniversary of the annual international Fajr Film Festival, held in Tehran and organized by the Farabi Cinema Foundation. In past years this event has attracted large numbers of foreigners to Tehran to witness newly-released Iranian films. Included in the list of visitors are a select group of guests who are the organizers of international film festivals. This past February, however, invitations issued to Western directors of international film festivals were canceled. For many observers, this represented the effects of the more restrictive policies taking hold since the 1992 resignation of former Minister of Culture and Islamic Guidance Mohammad Khatami.

Iranian films shown abroad must obtain a special permit from the Ministry of Culture and Islamic Guidance. The following are examples of films recently shown at international film festivals which have been previously censored in Iran.

• Bahram Beizai's *Bashu* was banned from 1986 to 1989. It received the First Prize at the Festival of "Art et Essai" Films for Children in Aubervilliers in 1990.

• Amir Naderi's *Ab, Bad, Khak* (Water, Wind, Dust) was banned from 1985 to 1989. It received the Grand Prix at the Fukuoka Asian Film Festival in 1991; the Bronze Prize at the Damascus Festival in 1991; First Prize at the Derde Festival in Bruges in 1990; and the Grand Prix at the Festival des Trois Continents in Nantes in 1989.

•Said Ebrahimifar's *Nar-o-Nay* (Pomegranate and Cane) was banned for two years from 1987-1989.[19] It received three awards at the 1989 Fajr Festival. It also received the Golden Tulip at the Istanbul Festival in 1990; and the Promotion Prize for Intercultural Dialogue at the Mannheim Film Days in 1989.

•Masud Kimiai's 1990 film *Dandan Mar* (Snake's Fang) was shortened under pressure from the censorship board.[20] It received the Special Jury Mention at Berlin Festival in 1991.

Similarly, many of the film directors invited to international festivals have been targets of the government's censorship policies, with the result that many of their films have been banned or revised. Noteworthy in this group are: Amir Naderi, Masud Kimiai, Bahram Beizai, Mohsen Makhmalbaf and Dariush Mehrjui. All but Naderi live and produce their films in Iran.

A conscious double standard is used to create a positive image of Iran abroad which is at odds with standards prevailing inside the country. For example, photographs of Susan Taslimi, who plays the main character Nai in the film *Bashu,* were prohibited on publicity posters inside Iran.[21] Yet the entire series of Iranian films screened at New York's Lincoln Center in November 1992 was introduced with the picture of Nai on festival posters and guide.[22] This same picture was used to promote the screening of *Bashu* at movie theaters in Rome in August 1991. Images of women for promotional purposes are a matter of much controversy in Iran, particularly in the case of Taslimi, who has been criticized for her nontraditional and central female roles.

On occasion, different versions of a film have been prepared for domestic and foreign use. The version of Rakhshan Bani-Etemad's film *Nargess* screened in Iran ends with a chorus of voices, while the version

---

[19] Young, "Iranian Cinema Now," p. 38.

[20] Ibid., p. 37.

[21] Miller, "Movies of Iran Struggle for Acceptance," p. 14.

[22] The semi-autonomous Farabi Cinema Foundation has exclusive control over the screening and promotion of Iranian films abroad.

screened abroad ends with the solo singing of a woman, which is prohibited in Iran. Similarly, the most recent film by Ibrahim Hatem Kia, *Az Karkheh Ta Rayn* (From Karkheh to the Rhine), which portrays the treatment of chemical weapon victims from the Iran-Iraq war in Germany, appears in two versions: one shot for domestic consumption with women wearing the Islamic headdress and the other for international use with women wearing wigs.

TWO BANNED FILM DIRECTORS

Bahram Beizai

The works of Bahram Beizai, one of Iran's best-known film directors, have been frequent targets of censorship, and he has been particularly vocal in criticizing censorship policies. His work often has come under attack for the central role given to women in his films, and for their traditional Persian themes. The fate of his most recent film *Mosaferan* (Travelers) shows the intricacy of government censorship, a mixture of government-imposed financial constraints and self-censorship.

Mosaferan portrays the transformation of a marriage ceremony into a funeral procession through a string of unfortunate events, notably a tragic car accident. Since his last film had been given an A ranking, he bypassed the script approval stage and presented his finished film to the Reviewing Council of the Ministry of Culture and Islamic Guidance. The Council required modification of a number of scenes in the film; these included adding the Koran to the funeral procession and deleting some of the joyful marriage scenes, especially those involving young women. Beizai objected to the requested modifications, stating that they were not workable without destroying the overall structure and content of the film. He later asked rhetorically in a publicly released letter to the Ministry, "Is it illegal to be happy?"

After a period of negotiations, the Council acquiesced to a shorter list of modifications with which Beizai complied, and a permit was issued to the film in August 1991. *Mosaferan* was screened for the first time at the Tenth Fajr Festival in February 1992 and given an award by the Ministry. The Ministry set the date for the public screening of the film to September 1992.

In June 1992, however, a representative from the Ministry contacted Beizai and asked him to request a postponement of the screening of *Mosaferan* to the winter schedule, since the *javv* was unstable, stating that "the motorcycle riders are in the street."[23] The winter schedule would have resulted in significantly reduced revenue and exposure. Beizai refused to request a postponement. In a November 1992 letter to the Ministry,[24] he later wrote:

> What does it mean that every day you read out a list of modifications, without any official order, so that no official document is involved, and require that we write it down by hand without any questions and then pursuant to that take things out of the film with our own hands?

Having previously issued an approval permit and even given an award to the film, the Ministry once again required extensive modification of *Mosaferan*. Beizai's letter to the Ministry complained of its censorship policies, the unreliability of laws and institutionalized self-censorship. He wrote:

> Instead of supporting us against this purported exterior *javv*, you have risen in support of it and have required that I implement five new deletions which amount in fact to many times more than five modifications.
>
> . . . If it is the *Keyhan* supporters, the writers of the magazine *Sureh*,[25] and motorcycle riders who determine

[23] The reference is to *hezbollahi*, or gangs of protesters, who frequently appear on motorcycles.

[24] The letter was published in Persian-language publications outside Iran, as well as photocopied and circulated hand-to-hand inside the country, and faxed abroad. Translation by Middle East Watch.

[25] *Sureh* is published by the Islamic Propagation Organization, a semi-autonomous foundation.

> the faith of our films, then why do we submit our films to you?
>
> . . . This *javv* is make-believe and false.

With this letter, Beizai returned the award given to him at the Tenth Fajr Festival and forbade the screening of his film abroad. *Mosaferan* was canceled at its scheduled screening at the November 1992 "Iranian Film Series" of The Film Society of Lincoln Center in New York.

Nonetheless, the film's censored version was screened in Tehran in February 1993 and during the winter schedule as desired by the Ministry. In view of the heavy costs that would have resulted from not showing the film, the three producers who had worked with Beizai arranged for the alteration and screening of the film in compliance with the Ministry's demands. Beizai, nevertheless, was left with a debt of 5.5 million tomans (approximately $ 32,000) after four years of work on *Mosaferan*.

Beizai's internationally acclaimed *Bashu, Garibeh-ye Kuchak* (Bashu the Little Stranger) was banned for three years, from 1986 to 1989, for being anti-war. His film *Shayad Vagthy Degar* (Maybe Some Other Time), released in 1992, was censored. Two of his other films, *Cherikheh Tara* (Ballad of Tara) and *Margh Yazdegerd* (Death of Yazdgerd), have been banned since 1979 and 1981, respectively, because women appear in them without head coverings, the strong central role of the female characters and the prominence of Persian themes.[26] Since 1980, his request to get a permit to work in theater has been denied for unknown reasons.

Beizai was not allowed to leave the country in September 1992 to attend the Toronto International Film Festival where his film *Bashu* was being screened.

Mohsen Makhmalbaf

Control and censorship are not the lot of the secular intellectuals alone. Mohsen Makhmalbaf, who entered the film industry since the revolution with a history of imprisonment under the Shah and strong

[26] Miller, "Movies of Iran Struggle for Acceptance," p. 14.

hezbollahi convictions, has had two of his recent films banned and a third censored. So uncompromising are the Islamic pressure groups that they have also aimed to impede and silence the work of this "insider" who has departed from their narrow definitions of acceptable conduct. The scenario is by now a familiar one. A litany of criticism populates the pages of the state-controlled media, an atmosphere of "public" outrage is fabricated and eventually pre-approved works are officially banned. At the core of these confrontations is a struggle of different factions for power.

Makhmalbaf's earlier works were hailed by the *hezbollahi* as a prime embodiment of revolutionary values by a truly Islamic film director. They included such films as *Tobeh Nosooh* (Nosooh's Repentance) in 1982, *Do Cheshm Be Soo* (Two Sightless Eyes) in 1983, *Este-azeh* (Seeking Sanctuary) in 1984, and *Bycott* (Boycott) in 1985. In later years, however, his work became increasingly realistic and socially critical.

By virtue of his established Islamic credentials, he was initially afforded liberties in his films that others with more secular leanings were flatly denied. But hard-liners' criticism mounted as he presented vivid and critical portrayals of the effects of abject poverty, and the disillusionment of soldiers with the Iran-Iraq war in his three subsequent films: *Dastforoush* (Peddler) in 1987, *Arusi-e Khuban* (Marriage of the Blessed) in 1989, and *Baysikel Ran* (Cyclist) in 1989. *Baysikel Ran* received the First Prize at the Rimini Cinema Festival in 1989. By then, however, Makhmalbaf was no longer granted any degree of immunity by the hard-line pressure groups.

Two of his later films -- *Nobat-e Asheghi* (Time for Love) in 1990 and *Shabhayeh Zayandeh Roud* (Nights of Zayandeh Roud) in 1991 -- came under extreme attack after their showing in 1991 at the Ninth Fajr Film Festival in Tehran. They were attacked for depicting physical or human love, and for undermining the values of the Islamic Revolution. Once again, *Keyhan* was in the lead in assaulting the character of the filmmaker, and the policies of the Ministry in particular, and the government in general. *Resalat, Jomhouri-ye Islami, Abrar* and to a lesser extent *Ettela'at* were also active in this campaign. Government officials, such as Ayatollah Ahmad Jannati, a member of the Council of Guardians, and Ali Akbar Nateq Nuri, speaker of the Majlis, also joined the chorus of discontent. The fact that Makhmalbaf has shaved his beard was also criticized by the press as signaling his break with the *hezbollahi*. The ringing reprise in the newspapers was: What has become of our Makhmalbaf?

In March 1991, in an open letter addressed to the media in response to their brutal "public prosecution" of him and his work, Makhmalbaf concluded with the following comment:

> The writer of these columns knows well that these arguments have nothing to do with him. The fight is over nothing other than the struggles between the different factions who seek power.
>
> The person who has more might is right. It is clear from now who the loser in this dispute is. Very well, congratulations. Who is the next person?[27]

Not all intellectuals, artists and government officials remained silent in this affair, and even some loyal advocates of the regime came to the defense of Makhmalbaf and his films. The magazine *Soroush,* the official organ of the Islamic Republic of Iran Broadcasting, appealed to the government to defend its policies in the face of the vilification campaign and remarked that because of the vilification, film, books, journals and music were under increased pressures.[28] Former Minister of Culture and Islamic Guidance Mohammad Khatami condemned the tyranny of a single narrow viewpoint, and accused Ayatollah Jannati of undermining artists' peace of mind and work.[29] Dr. Abdol Karim Soroush, a renowned Islamic scholar and lecturer, also spoke in defense of the artist and his work and encouraged people not to be swayed by the "propaganda of fascists."[30]

In this particular battle, the voice and power of the more intolerant factions prevailed and both of Makhmalbaf's films were banned. His 1993 film *Honarpisheh* (Actor), was issued a release permit

---

[27] *Film,* March/April 1991, p. 125. Translation by Middle East Watch.

[28] Golmakani, "New Times, Same Problems," p. 22.

[29] *Film,* June/July 1991, p. 88.

[30] Ibid., p. 93.

only after certain portions were censored.[31] And the proposed screenplay for his most recent work, involving the Iraqi occupation of Kuwait, was rejected.[32] The banning and censorship of these works, however, has not prevented the government from allowing the screening of his other recent film *Nasseredin Shah Actor-e Cinema* (Once upon a Time Cinema) at international festivals, where it won three prizes in 1992.

---

[31] *Hamshahri*, January 9, 1993, p. 20.

[32] *Film*, May/June 1993, p. 12. The screenplay was rejected by the Council of Screenplay Inspection for three reasons: (1) it portrayed Iraq as too much of an aggressor, and Kuwait as too much of a victim; (2) it portrayed the West as liberators; and (3) it did not sufficiently convey the innocence of the Shi'a people. Ibid.

9
BANNED POLITICAL EXPRESSION

All forms of political expression and dissent are strictly curtailed as undermining the prevailing system of governance based on *velayat-i-faqih*. Coupled with this ban on political discourse, large numbers of political prisoners have been executed and imprisoned since the revolution, the precise numbers of whom are unknown.[1] While many political organizations joined hands to bring about the revolution in 1979, political opposition was abruptly and violently curbed soon after the establishment of the Islamic Republic. Due to the government's repressive policies, almost all dissident political groups have been forced to continue their activities in exile.

All forms of expression and speech associated with opposition movements were proscribed in the first years after the revolution. For example, in 1980 and 1981, the ruling clerics cracked down on news organs of former allies: *Mojahed*, the newspaper of the People's Mojahedin Khalq Organization of Iran, *Mizan* (Scales of Justice), the newspaper of the *Nehzat-e-Azadi-ye Iran* (Iranian Freedom Movement) and *Enqelab-e Eslami* (Islamic Revolution), the newspaper of former President Abolhassan Bani-Sadr. In 1983, the government banned *Mardom* (People), the newspaper of the communist Tudeh party.

Shabnamehs, or clandestine political publications, are distributed irregularly in Iran, at high risk to their publishers and distributors. Among them are open letters by Dr. Mehdi Bazargan, the first Prime Minister of post-revolutionary Iran, on behalf of his Iranian Freedom Movement. These letters regularly attack the government's policies, notably on freedom of expression and politial association, but also on such issues as the raising of foreign loans. Occasionally these statements have been published, in part, in the recognized media; more often they are circulated clandestinely in xeros form.

---

[1] It is extremely difficult to be precise about these cases. However, Amnesty International has estimated at least 2,500 political executions in 1988, the highest number for any year since the immediate post-revolutionary period. For 1991, AI documented 775 executions, of which at least sixty were the result of convictions on political charges; and for 1992, 330 executions of which at least 140 of the executed had been formally charged with political offenses.

Reprisals Against Publications

The most recent publications attacked or banned on political grounds are the following:

•On May 14, 1993, a group of motorcycle riders attacked the office of the scientific magazine *Kiyan* and broke windows in the facility.[2] Islamic Revolutionary Guards (*Pasdaran*) did not intervene until the computer system and files had been damaged. The attackers called for the death of the magazine's editor, Reza Tehrani, and demanded that the magazine be closed because of an interview it had published with Bazargan, in which they claimed he had insulted Islam. The government has taken no action against the attackers, but Tehrani was questioned by the Islamic Revolutionary Prosecutor's Office. The magazine is still permitted to publish.

•In April 1993, a special court of the clergy[3] banned the magazine *Rah-e Mojahed* (The Path of the Mojahed) published by Lotfollah Meissami for including statements by Ayatollah Hossein Ali Montazeri's aides denouncing attacks on his office and his followers the previous February.[4] Ayatollah Montazeri, the appointed successor to Ayatollah Khomeini until 1989, is now an opponent and critic of Supreme Religious Leader Ayatollah Khamenei and President Rafsanjani. A number of Montazeri's aides, including his son-in-law, was arrested and their offices ransacked in February 1993 after he gave a speech to his theology class in Qom criticizing the Iranian leadership.

•In early 1991, Abolfazl Mussavian, a religious personality, journalist and editor of the local daily *Khorasan* in Mashhad, was arrested. He had published an article about Ayatollah Montazeri. He was accused of publishing "lies liable to disturb public order" and of writing material contrary to Ayatollah Khomeini's edicts. He was convicted following a

---

[2] IRNA, May 15, 1993 as reported in FBIS, May 19, 1993.

[3] The special court of the clergy investigates offenses by clerics. It was instituted in 1987 on the decree of Ayatollah Khomeini.

[4] Reuters, April 28 1993; and *Iran Times*, May 7, 1993, p. 6.

secret summary trial before a special court for the clergy, and sentenced to one year imprisonment and punishment by whipping. In October 1991 his sentence was commuted to internal exile in a village near Qom. He has reportedly completed his term of banishment and is now living in Mashhad.

The number of persons imprisoned or executed in connection with their non-violent expression of political dissent is not known. Out of fear for their own and their families' well-being, many known victims do not publicize their cases. The persecution of three women writers and journalists associated with the communist Tudeh Party, however, has received much international attention. The three were imprisoned in 1983, before the party was outlawed; they were tried summarily and convicted in 1986. The charges brought against them are not known. They are:

•Mariam Firouz, a prominent writer, editor, and translator in her late seventies. She is the author of an autobiography, *Familiar Faces*, and was chief editor of the magazine *Jahan-e Zanan* (Women's World). Previously imprisoned during the time of the Shah, after the revolution she was imprisoned again and given a death sentence, later commuted to an indefinite prison term. While in prison, she was tortured. Since 1991, there are reports that she has been transferred to a guarded facility outside of the prison compound, where she is receiving medical care, but she continues to suffer from ill health. In this compound she has been permitted to live with her long-time companion, Noureddine Kianouri, the former First Secretary of the outlawed Tudeh Party -- also imprisoned since 1983 and in poor health.

•Malakeh Mohammadi, a prominent journalist and editor in her late seventies. She was the editor of the Tudeh party newspapers *Mardom* (People) and *Donya* (World). In 1986 she received a death sentence, later commuted to an indefinite prison term. She reportedly was tortured in prison. Since 1991, there are reports that she has been released and is presently under house arrest.

•Zohreh Ghaeni, an editor in her thirties. She was the editor of a young women's newspaper, *Azzaraksh*. Previously imprisoned during the time of the Shah, after the revolution she was sentenced to eight years. She was reportedly released from prison in 1991.

Article 26 of the Constitution provides for the right to political association.[5] The Political Parties Act, ratified on August 29, 1981, sets out conditions for the formation of parties, societies and other associations and dictates the guidelines for processing a permit by the Ministry of the Interior.

Despite these provisions, the list of organizations allowed to register consists mainly of such nonpolitical groups as the Islamic Association of Graduates from the Indo-Pakistan Sub-Continent, the Society of Zoroastrian Priests, the Society of Surgeons, the Association of Pediatricians, the Association for Women of the Islamic Republic and the Islamic Center of Teachers. The only political groupings permitted are different factions of the clergy, such as the Tehran Combatant Clergy Association (the original group) (*Majma'-e Rowhaniyat-e Mobarez-e Tehran*), and the Tehran Combatant Clergy Association (the breakaway group) (*Majma'-e Rowhaniyun-e Mobarez-e Tehran*). No political parties exist.

The two sister organizations profiled below are the only ones that officially remain in Iran. The reprisals against their activists for the exercise of Constitutionally protected speech have received wide international attention.[6]

---

[5] Article 26 reads:

> The formation of parties, societies, political or professional associations, as well as religious societies, whether Islamic or pertaining to one of the recognized religious minorities, is permitted provided they do not violate the principles of independence, freedom, national unity, the criteria of Islam, or the basis of the Islamic Republic. No one may be prevented from participating in the aforementioned groups, or be compelled to participate in them.

[6] See, for example, Middle East Watch, "Iran: Political Dissidents, Held for Over a Year, Are Reportedly Sentenced." (New York: 1991).

POLITICAL DISSIDENTS PUNISHED

Nehzat-e Azadi (Freedom Movement) and its sister organization, *Jamiyat Defa Az Azadi va Hakemiyat Mellat Iran* (Association for the Defense of Freedom and the Sovereignty of the Iranian Nation, ADFSIN) established in 1961 and 1986 respectively, are the only opposition groups that officially have remained in Iran and continued their activities, despite numerous failed attempts to obtain political permits. Both organizations are led by Mehdi Bazargan, Iran's first Prime Minister after the revolution. The organizations' members have been repeatedly imprisoned and their offices ransacked for the nonviolent expression of their beliefs. The Freedom Movement's newspaper *Mizan* (Scales of Justice) has been banned since 1981.

In May 1988, eight political activists associated with the Freedom Movement and the ADFSIN were taken into custody after they and others addressed an open letter to Ayatollah Khomeini and issued a leaflet calling for an end to the eight-year Iran-Iraq war. Three activists arrested at this time -- Ali Ardalan, Shah Hoseyni and Mohammad Tavassoli -- were held until the ceasefire was declared in July 1988. On June 1, 1988, the offices of the organization were occupied and closed by the Islamic Revolutionary Prosecutor's Office, their books and files confiscated. The newspapers *Jomhouri-ye Islami* and *Keyhan* announced that pursuant to the order of the Revolutionary Prosecutor of Tehran, the persons arrested were "nationalist elements" who had sided with "global arrogance," engaged in pro-Iraq propaganda and had "offended the honorable families of the martyrs."[7]

In June 1990, twenty-five political activists associated with the Freedom Movement and ADFSIN, some of whom had suffered imprisonment under the Shah, were taken into custody once again after they and sixty-five other prominent Iranians signed an open letter to President Ali Akbar Hashemi Rafsanjani criticizing his government's domestic and foreign policies and demanding greater civil liberties. On August 6, Dr. Farhad Behbahani, one of the detainees and a member of the Central Council of the Freedom Movement, was forced into a staged public confession on national television about the association's "opposition to the system of the Islamic Republic of Iran" and "very strong intellectual

---

[7] See, e.g., *Keyhan*, June 4, 1988.

and moral affinity with America." Behbahani was subsequently released from prison but since then has been prevented from working.

Sixteen of the group were released during the year following their arrest. Nine, however, remained in custody and were sentenced in June 1991 after a closed hearing, without benefit of legal counsel and without being informed of the official charges against them. They were accused by Iranian officials and the state-owned media of contact and collaboration with foreign powers.

The nine persons and their sentences consist of: Hashem Sabbaghian (six months); Mohammad Tavassoli Hojati and Abdolali Bazargan (two years); and Habibollah Davaran, Khosrow Mansourian, Akbar Zarinehbaf, Ali Ardalan, Nezameldin Movahed and Abolfazl Mirshams Shahshahani (three years). Due to his poor health, Ali Ardalan was transferred to Jam Hospital in Tehran. The others remained in Tehran's Evin prison. Their sentences commenced from the date of the hearing despite the nearly one year of incarceration beforehand. In April 1992, on the occasion of the thirteenth anniversary of the founding of the Islamic Republic, all nine were pardoned and released.

Since passage of the Political Parties Act in 1981, both the Freedom Movement and the ADFSIN have applied for licenses in accordance with the law. Pursuant to Article 14 of the Political Parties Act, they repeatedly have confirmed their allegiance to the Constitution of the Islamic Republic of Iran.[8] Until August 1992, there was no official response to their numerous requests; nor had the organizations been declared illegal.

In a statement issued on August 9, 1992, the Interior Ministry stated that "after much deliberation" by the Commission of Article 10,[9]

---

[8] Pursuant to Article 14 of the Political Parties Act, all groups requesting a permit must declare in their bylaws their allegiance to the Constitution of the Islamic Republic of Iran.

[9] This Commission is instituted pursuant to Article 10 of the Political Parties Act. Within ten days of receiving a request for a permit, the Ministry of the Interior is required to submit the request to the Commission for consideration and determination (Art. 9). The Commission comprises a representative from the General Prosecutor's Office; a representative of the Supreme Judicial Council; a representative of the Ministry of the Interior, and two representatives of the *Majlis* (Art. 10). The commissioners serve two-year terms.

the Freedom Movement's request had been denied. Pursuant to Article 13 of the act,[10] the Freedom Movement filed a complaint with the First Civil Court of Tehran on October 15, 1992 contesting the legality of the Commission's ruling. Basing its case on Article 168 of the Constitution,[11] it has requested a jury trial. At this writing, there has been no official action on the complaint.

Meanwhile, the activities of the Freedom Movement and the ADFSIN continue. They issue letters, leaflets and newsletters which appear in irregular intervals and are distributed through volunteer networks. The independent magazine *Iran-e Farda* (Iran of Tomorrow) often voices the views of the Freedom Movement, for which it is frequently the object of harsh criticism in the hard-line press.

---

[10] Article 15(2) of the Political Parties Act provides that within a month from the time that the Commission of Article 10 rejects a request for a permit, the rejected group can file a complaint with the court. The court is required to respond within three months.

[11] Article 168 of the Constitution reads in part: "Political and press offenses will be tried openly and in the presence of a jury, in courts of justice."

10
RESTRICTED ACADEMIC FREEDOM[1]

Soon after the 1979 change of government, universities that had previously been nerve centers of the revolution became areas where the new regime sought to suppress political dissent and consolidate its power. In June 1980, armed gangs of hooligans loyal to the hard-line clergy assaulted campuses with the proclaimed goal of closing the offices of university political groups. These brutal attacks, which lasted for three days, were carried out with the acquiescence and tacit approval of the authorities. In their wake were scores of dead and injured students. The incident marked the end of eighteen months of relative freedom of association and debate on university campuses.

Following these attacks, universities were officially closed for two years in order to produce a "cultural revolution" in every aspect of their operation. On June 3, 1980, the Setad-e Enqelab-e Farhangi (Cultural Revolution Panel) appointed by Ayatollah Khomeini was given the task of "Islamicizing" the faculty, students and curricula of all primary and secondary schools and universities. Textbooks in law, social sciences and the humanities were rewritten according to Islamic canons.

Faculties and students were purged, detained, executed or forced into exile. According to the Minister of Culture and Higher Education, the number of university professors and lecturers teaching in Iran's thirty-four universities and other institutions of higher learning dropped from 12,000 before the revolution to 6,000 by 1989.[2] Overall more than 60,000 teachers were purged on the basis of their political beliefs.[3] Many of these academics were branded lackeys of imperialism, Shah-lovers, spies, Freemasons, Zionists, Baha'is, leftists and infidels.

In October 1981, the government started incrementally reopening universities. A seven-member Supreme Council of Cultural Revolution appointed by Ayatollah Khomeini supervises university affairs.

---

[1] This section is a general overview of the academic environment in Iran. A comprehensive understanding of the mechanisms of government control and manipulation of this environment requires further study.

[2] *Washington Post*, November 5, 1989. (This official is not to be confused with the Minister of Culture and Islamic Guidance.)

[3] *Iran Times*, February 22, 1991, p. 5.

Politicized Admissions

The student body also faced various discriminatory practices. After passing rigorous country-wide entrance examinations and regardless of their academic qualifications, students had to pass a "character" test before securing entry into a university. These practices started once the universities reopened.[4] The government investigates an applicant's religious, family and ideological background and political activities. The investigators inquire, among other things, whether the prospective student prays, participates in political rallies, goes to Friday prayers and observes the Islamic dress code. If these investigations reveal anything that is viewed with disfavor, the student is barred from attending university. Reports from Iran indicate that this practice has abated in the past five years for entrance into undergraduate programs, while it still persists for graduate and post-graduate programs.

Universities are further impeded by far-reaching government quotas. According to President Rafsanjani, approximately forty percent of student admittance is devoted to released prisoners of war, the revolutionary guards, paramilitary volunteers (*basijis*) and the families of martyrs from the revolution and the war with Iraq.[5] These students are offered exclusive summer classes, private tutoring, scholarships, extra bonus points and a specially designed entrance exam to facilitate their admission. The semi-autonomous foundation Bonyad Shohada (Martyr's Foundation) even established its own special primary and secondary schools to serve these constituencies.[6]

Students ardently committed to the values of the revolution and the Islamic government are therefore assured a place on university campuses. They also serve as the "eyes and ears" of the authorities and report on those teachers and fellow students suspected of harboring anti-Islamic or anti-regime sentiments. As a Tehran University professor stated in 1992:

---

[4] See Appendix B for the accounts of three students who lost their places in university based on character tests in 1981, 1982 and 1983-84.

[5] *Iran Times*, December 6, 1991.

[6] *Keyhan Hava'i*, February 27, 1991, p. 17.

> They [students who entered through quotas] are all very fanatical in their views and create an atmosphere of fear in the classrooms. No secular ideas can be objectively presented and argued on university campuses. There have been many instances when these students have threatened their professors and demanded that they must abide by the Islamic principles in teaching and interpretation of their subject matters. On the other hand, even Islamic laws, theology and jurisprudence must be interpreted in accordance with the policies of the government. These students are very effective in keeping everybody in check, and . . . shut up everyone even in the university's classrooms.[7]

In a speech on December 10, 1992, addressing the "spread of Western infrastructure" in university curricula, Supreme Religious Leader Khamenei stated:

> Sciences that encompass Islamic thought and guidance must not be set aside in the universities. Without a doubt, students with Islamic credentials must be honored. The officials involved must put teaching of humanities based on Islamic thought and world outlook at the top of their agenda.[8]

Vigilance and Reprisals

The student organization Anjoman-Eslami Daneshjuyan (Islamic Association of Students) is composed of the hezbollahi group committed to monitoring the university atmosphere. It takes direct part in the administration of universities through the presence of its representatives on university control boards. The other, much less influential and younger student organization, *Jahad Daneshgahi* (Islamic Society of

---

[7] Middle East Watch interview.

[8] IRIB Television First Program Network, December 10, 1992, as reported in FBIS, December 11, 1992.

Students), is relatively moderate and engages in a variety of religious and cultural activities.

It is not uncommon for the Islamic Association of Students to threaten or complain about professors and prompt the university officials to reprimand or discharge them for being insufficiently Islamic. For example:

• In December 1992, students in the Islamic Association accused a professor at the Ahvaz College of Physical Education of "insulting Islamic values by drawing a caricature and displaying it in the college's poster area."[9] A statement issued by the students threatened: "If steps are not taken quickly we will act ourselves and give the proper answer to this insult and boldness."[10] The president of the university promised to take appropriate measures in response.

• In November 1992, students in the Islamic Association complained about Professor Jafar-Poor in the Free University of Tehran and accused him of "insulting sacred things and the beliefs of Muslims."[11] At issue was a joke he made in class that, due to technological innovations, it was now possible to exchange the air in heaven with that in hell. In response to the complaint, Jafar-Poor was discharged from the university.

Restrictions for Women

Female students have had to contend with even more severe restrictions on their access to education than their male colleagues. According to the January 1993 report of Reynaldo Galindo Pohl, the Special Representative of the U.N. Commission on Human Rights for Iran, out of 169 fields of study in higher education women are banned from ninety-one. These include fifty-five fields out of eighty-four in technology and mathematics, seven out of forty in natural sciences, from

---

[9] London *Keyhan*, December 24, 1992, p. 5, as reported in FBIS, January 12, 1993.

[10] Ibid.

[11] *Iran Times*, March 19, 1993.

all four fields of agriculture, and twenty-five out of thirty-five in the faculty of letters and humanities. In its response to the Special Representative in February 1993, the Islamic Republic of Iran stated that there were "no limitations on women to attain professional positions or to continue their studies, and only infrequently are recommendations made to female students concerning a limited number of fields of study."[12] In reality, binding restrictions in Iran often occur in the stated form of "recommendation" and "advice."

[12] Iran Response to U.N. Feb. 1993 at para. 28.

11
DENIAL AND DISTORTION OF CULTURAL HERITAGE

After the revolution, the victorious Shi'a clerics initially set out to downplay ancient Persian customs, artifacts and heritage, reversing the Shah's emphasis on Iran's pre-Islamic and monarchical history. Not only were they dedicated to fighting Western cultural hegemony but they were also determined to sever or weaken all ties to pre-Islamic values and ideas. This campaign has been largely unsuccessful due to public resistance. Yet it comes to the fore from time to time.

In the early revolutionary period, many of Iran's museums and private collections and archives were despoiled, auctioned off or endangered through neglect or inadequate preservation. In line with their clear preference for Iran's Islamic period, the government discouraged any archeological excavation of pre-Islamic sites on the grounds that all that was to be found were relics of the age of idolatry. The more fanatical factions opted for extirpating all mausoleums and icons they deemed to be non-Islamic. Soon after the revolution, bands of hooligans attacked symbols of Iran's monarchical past, such as the ancient ruins of Persepolis, the Safavid-era bathhouse of Khosrow Khan, and the pre-Islamic Ganj-nameh, an adored petroglyph in Hamadan. The Iranian Cultural Heritage Organization, affiliated with the Ministry of Culture and Higher Education, is now vested with the responsibility to safeguard such national treasures.

Similarly, the ruling clerics decided to remove or simply replace all allusions to kings in Iranian popular lexicon. The names of all cities, streets or monuments referring to any Shahs or monarchical dynasties were changed. As examples of this revolutionary nomenclature, Masjed-e Shah (Shah's Mosque) and Maidan-e Shah (Shah's Square) in Isfahan and the port city of Bandar Abbas (named for Shah Abbas) were respectively renamed Masjed-e Imam (Imam's Mosque), Maiden-e Imam (Imam's Square) and Bandar Khomeini.

In order to further "cleanse" the popular vocabulary the government has restricted the range of names parents can choose to name their children. Names and titles with a royal connotation or those that are judged demeaning of exalted religious personalities are prohibited when obtaining birth certificates. The use of Arabic, the original language of the Koran, in place of the equivalent Persian words has gained much currency since the revolution.

This process of "Islamicizing" Iran's cultural heritage has left perhaps its most enduring imprint on the educational system and the younger generation of Iranians coming of age since the revolution. The government-sanctioned revision of history that is prevalent in lower-school textbooks ranges from exaggerating or distorting the role of Islam in bringing about historic milestones, such as the nationalization of the Iranian oil industry in the late 1940's, to negative characterizations of Iran's former kings, especially all aspects of the reigns of Reza Shah and Mohammand Reza Shah.[1] The role of the clergy in Iranian history is also presented in distorted form. History textbooks fail to acknowledge the symbiotic relationship that existed for centuries between the clergy and the monarchy and foreign powers (e.g. Russia and Britain) in Iran. Similarly, ignored is the certain influential clerics' role in opposing the constitutional movement in early 1900's and in supporting the Qajar monarchy.

Literary giants whose work is not in line with the prevailing value system have been either outright banned, de-emphasized or reinterpreted. The hedonistic poetry of Omar Khayyam, the Sufi poetry of Nasser Khosrow, the classical poetry of Hafez and the *Shah Nameh* (The Book of Kings) of Hakim Abolqasem Ferdowsi are among such works.[2]

The publication history of the *Divan*, by the poet Mohammad-Taqi Bahar ("Malek-al-So'ara"), demonstrates a practice employed by successive Iranian governments -- the manipulation and distortion of literary and historical works to serve political ends.[3] Since first appearing fifty years ago, the *Divan* has gone through four editions, and each time its content has been altered to conform with the prevailing political climate. During the previous regime, it was censored so as to remove all allusions to the poet's opposition to and criticism of Reza Shah's rule. The post-revolutionary regime conversely added previously deleted poems to the fourth edition printed in 1989, while deleting such poems as *Ey Zan* and *Chahar Ketaba*, in which Bahar supported women's freedom and criticized religious fanaticism.

---

[1] Jalal Matini, "Negating the Past," *Index on Censorship* (June 1985), pp. 42-45.

[2] Ferdowsi is the man credited with reviving both the Persian language and Iranian nationalism in the tenth century after years of domination by Arabs and Islam.

[3] Ahmad Karimi-Hakkak, "Censorship," *Encyclopedia Iranica* (1990), p. 141.

However, the public's resistance has forced the government to back down in certain respects. In a significant act of reversal, the millennium anniversary of Ferdowsi's *Shah Nameh* in December 1990 was celebrated by an officially-organized international conference. A similar reversal is evident in the Iranian New Year celebrations, *Nowruz*, and a Persian festival celebrating autumn, *Mehregan*. While initially such traditions were downplayed in favor of religious occasions, this changed in March 1990: for the first time since the revolution, the government celebrated the Iranian new year, and Ayatollah Khamenei even spoke about the importance of the occasion and the traditions attached to it.[4]

There are no guarantees that such liberalization will last, however. In 1992, after years of trying to suppress the ancient Zoroastrian "fire festival" *Chahar Shanbeh Soori*, the government for the first time allowed the festivities to occur. *Chahar Shanbeh Soori*, an old Persian tradition celebrated right before the New Year, is considered pagan by the ruling clergy. Then, in March 1993, came a new government crackdown. Anti-riot police detained hundreds of youths in Tehran setting off firecrackers and lighting fires to celebrate the festival.[5] Media reports stated that a possible reason for the government's reaction may have been that the festival coincided this year with the period of mourning for Imam Ali, one of the principal religious leaders for Muslims.

---

[4] *Middle East International*, March 30, 1990, p. 4.

[5] Agence France Presse, March 17, 1993.

CONCLUSION

In any society, the principal guardians of free expression are individual artists and intellectuals who push the limits of permissible discourse and challenge the predominant ideology. The range of critical and opposing views expressed, the diversity of speakers represented and the costs attached to artistic and intellectual endeavor are the measure of freedom in a society. In Iran the parameters for discourse are strictly defined, and the range of speakers is limited to the various factions of the ruling elite. The punishment for deviation from these parameters in turn can be severe, ranging from the destruction or confiscation of property, harassment and financial ruin, to prosecution, imprisonment and even death.

The findings of this report in relation to the different arenas of expression are summarized below:

•The press in Iran, compared with some countries in the region, presents a range of views, but the scope of permissible dissent or criticism is nevertheless extremely narrow, limited to partisans of the ruling movement. All newspapers and some magazines are either owned by or closely affiliated with the government. Independent magazines are generally precluded from covering the political arena and from overt social criticism. Furthermore, the journalistic community is constantly plagued by the prospect of unchecked attacks by vigilante groups, prosecution based on the content of their published work, and imprisonment.

• Access of foreign journalists to Iran has increased since the end of the Iran-Iraq war in 1988. Nevertheless, in the case of "undersirable" news stories, foreign journalists in Iran still risk questioning by the government, closure of local offices and deportation. Iranian journalists working for foreign news agencies, moreover, are considered a suspect group by the authorities and are particularly vulnerable to government pressure.

•The crucial media of radio and television remain under government control and broadcast largely political and religious programs. No opposing or critical views from outside the governing elite find a voice on radio or television. Even debates on dissension within government circles is not broadcast.

• Books are plentiful and give voice to relatively diverse opinions. But a cumbersome and arbitrary system of book censorship allows the government to control, alter and ban work whenever it wishes. Hard-sought government permits to publish a book provide no guarantee for its continued existence; nor do they provide for the security of its author and others associated with its publication in the face of unchecked vigilante attacks. Content-based prosecutions and imprisonment may occur whether or not a book has been officially approved. The financial loss represented by books banned after publication serves as an effective tool of government retribution and increases the pressures for self-censorship.

• Since its issuance in February 1989, the *fatwa* has been reconfirmed by leading members of the Iranian government. The bounty offered by the semi-autonomous Fifteenth of Khordad Foundation has been increased for the third time from $2 million dollars to an undetermined amount. Additionally, the *fatwa* has been extended to increasing numbers of individuals who have dared to speak out against the death threat and in support of freedom of expression. The group of 162 Iranians in exile who issued a declaration condemning the *fatwa* at their personal risk and cost is a notable example.

• Iranian films have received international praise in the past decade. But for all the individual foreign success stories, proportionately far more screenplays have been rejected, and films banned or censored, including the work of filmmakers who are internationally acclaimed. As with books, government permits for films are meaningless in the face of a critical or unsympathetic "public atmosphere" or *javv*. This *javv* is often whipped up artificially by vigilante groups and intolerant factions within the ruling elite; yet it is customary for government officials to alter state policy in response to the prevailing *javv*. The financial loss involved in having a film banned also serves as a tool of control and censorship.

• Political speech that is genuinely independent or critical of the government persists only on the margins of the society. The government deals with any infringement in this domain decisively and with severity. Some underground publications and leaflets circulate clandestinely, but at a high risk to their authors and distributors.

•The academic environment is treated as an ideological training ground. Faculty and curricula have been "purged" and "Islamicized" since the revolution. Universities, in particular, are largely restricted to students with the "proper" ideological orientation, as interpreted by the government.

•Since the revolution, historical, literary and cultural texts have been rewritten to comply with Islamic criteria. Until recently the celebration of historic traditions, such as the New Year festivities, has been impeded by the government as remnants of Iran's pre-Islamic past and the age of idolatry. While the government's campaign has been largely unsuccessful due to public resistance, certain of its elements persist and come to the fore from time to time.

Furthermore, the laws in the Islamic Republic of Iran, as enacted and enforced, provide no guarantee of freedom of expression, and no protection to those who exceed the narrow confines of accepted discourse. The Constitution's guarantee of freedom of expression is crippled by exceptions that require compliance with "the fundamental principles of Islam or the rights of the public." The Press Law and film and book regulations expand on these debilitating exceptions. Provisions in these legal instruments, apart from setting the limits for discourse, also dictate its content; it is the duty of every citizen in all aspects of his or her life "to enjoin the good and forbid the evil," a Koranic phrase requiring every individual to lead a moral life. Additionally, eligibility to start a publication is limited by the Press Law to those who exhibit "moral fitness," as determined by the government. The Iranian government's enforcement of its laws is very selective. The Constitutional provision stating that "political and press offenses will be tried openly and in the presence of a jury, in courts of justice," and the Press Law's requirement that the Ministry of Culture and Islamic Guidance alone monitor press-related matters have been largely ignored. Instead, a number of different state (e.g. the Islamic Revolutionary Prosecutor) and state-affiliated (e.g. foundations and newspapers) entities maintain a tight hold on public expression. Similarly, despite provisions in the Press Law prohibiting defamation, libel and vilification, these obnoxious practices are a trademark of state-affiliated press attacks, particularly against the artistic and intellectual community. The provision of the Press Law categorically outlawing government censorship and control over the press is simply ignored.

In any event, a large part of the government's mechanisms of control and censorship fall outside the law. The government exercises control "unofficially" through binding "suggestions" and "advice" conveyed verbally, not in writing, to the responsible parties; or indirectly through the imposition of financial constraints and the unchecked reign of vigilante groups. In not a single case has the government sought to prosecute individuals who have taken the law into their own hands, destroyed property or threatened lives. On occasion, the government has even taken its cue from radical Islamic vigilante groups, as though they somehow articulated "public will," and has gone on to initiate its own prosecution of writers, cartoonists, publishers or editors.

The Iranian government's conduct in different arena of expression betrays an underlying belief that, through the close monitoring and restriction of information, it can control the thoughts of its citizens and secure the dominance of a prescribed set of values. In an ever-shrinking globe, in which the transfer and exchange of information respects no national boundaries, the Iranian government's efforts to maintain control of the public's access to information and images is ultimately a losing battle. Radio broadcasts, satellite communication, videos and facsimile machines, as well as the movement of people, ensure that the Iranian public's link with the outside world is not severed. It is no longer a question of whether the public will have access but rather through what medium. The government's repressive policies have merely deepened the people's distrust in, and indifference toward, the official media of information exchange.

It is in such an environment that Iranian women and men have continued to work and produce in their chosen medium, be it literature, film, art or music and to push the limits of freedom and challenge the reign of a prescribed set of values. Their work as well as their person or lives, however, bear the mark of their daily struggles against censorship, uncertainty and fear. The perseverance and determination of those committed to freedom -- freedom to think, speak, write and live as one chooses -- have not been without avail, and are at the basis of the relatively improved circumstances at the time of the publication of this report, over fourteen years after the revolution. Essential to the ideal of a free human being, however, is freedom from fear, and this the Iranian artist or intellectual is denied as she or he continues to lead a precarious existence in a society where the order of the day is arbitrariness. This report honors the courage of their struggles and the strength of their convictions.

APPENDIX A
DECLARATION OF IRANIAN INTELLECTUALS AND ARTISTS CONDEMNING THE *FATWA* AND SIGNATORIES AS OF MARCH 1993

Issued to the Iranian and international press in March 1992 to mark the third anniversary of the *fatwa*, the following declaration was the first collective statement by Iranians willing to lend their names in support of Salman Rushdie's right to life and free expression. The original fifty signatories appear here with asterisks following their names.

* * *

It is three years since Khomeini issued his death sentence against the writer, Salman Rushdie, and as yet no firm and decisive action has been taken by Iranians to condemn this inhuman decree. As this attack on the freedom of expression originated in Iran, we believe that Iranian intellectuals have a special responsibility forcefully to condemn this decree and to defend Salman Rushdie.

We, the signatories of this declaration, who in the past, individually and in many different ways, have shown [our] support for Salman Rushdie, believe that freedom of speech is one of the most precious of the achievements of mankind and that, as Voltaire remarked, this freedom would be meaningless unless individuals had the freedom to blaspheme. No one and no group has the right to limit this freedom in the name of one or another religion or sanctity.

We consider Khomeini's decree intolerable and emphasize that only esthetic criteria are valid in judging a work of art.

We unanimously raise our voices in the defense of Salman Rushdie. We call the world's attention to the fact that all Iranian writers, artists, journalists and thinkers inside Iran live daily under the merciless pressure of religious censorship and that the number of those who have been imprisoned or executed for "blasphemy" is not negligible.

We are convinced that silence and indifference towards the systematic violation of the most basic of human rights of the people of Iran cannot but embolden the Islamic Republic to implement worldwide its terroristic ideas and to issue decrees such as pronounced against Salman Rushdie.

1. Shahnaz AALAMI (Poet)*
2. Mahasti AFSHAR (Scholar)*
3. Kourosh AFSHARPANAH (Actor)

4. Shirzad AGHAIE (Poet)
5. Fereydoun AHMAD (Writer)
6. Reza ALLAMEH-ZADEH (Film-maker)*
7. Nasrin ALMASI (Actress)
8. Mahshid AMIR-SHAHI (Writer)*
9. Mishaneh AMIR-SHAHI (Scholar)*
10. Mansour ANVARI (Journalist)*
11. Mary APICK (Actress)
12. Ali-Mohammad ARBABI (Journalist)*
13. Aref AREFKIA (Vocalist)
14. Kourosh ARIA-MANESH (Scholar)*
15. Mina ASADI (Poet)
16. Bijan ASSADI-POUR (Caricaturist)*
17. Touraj ATABAKI (Scholar)*
18. Assur-Banipal BABELA (Dramatist)
19. Houshang BAHARLOU (Cinematographer)*
20. Mahmoud BAGHBAN (Artist/Photographer)
21. Behrouz BEHNEZAD (Actor)
22. Shahin BEHRAVESH (Psychologist)*
23. Ali-Asghar BEHROUZIAN (Writer)
24. Shahram BROUKHIM (Actor)
25. Jamshid CHALANGI (Writer)
26. Mohi CHAICHI (Actor)
27. Fereydoun DAEMI (Radio Programmer)
28. Hayadeh DARAGAHI (Scholar)
29. Ali DASTA (Actor)
30. Mahmoud DAVOUDI (Poet)
31. Mohammad-Reza DJALILI (Scholar)*
32. Mehrangiz DOWLATSHAHI (Sociologist)*
33. Farideh EBLAGHIAN (Writer)
34. Ahmad EBRAHIMI (Poet)
35. Homa EHSAN (Journalist/Radio producer)
36. Sadreldine ELAHI (Journalist/Novelist)*
37. Nasser EMAMI (Sculptor)
38. Nasser ENGHETAE (Journalist)
39. Ahmad ESFANDIAR-MAZ (Artist)
40. Khanak ESHGHI-SANATI (Lawyer)
41. Azar FAKHR (Actress)
42. Nasser FAKHTEH (Journalist)

43. Hossein FARAJI (Journalist)
44. Cyrous FARMANFARMAIAN (Architect)*
45. Farhang FARAHI (Journalist)*
46. Faramarz FARSHAD (Journalist)
47. Hamid FATEMI (Journalist)
48. Shahla FATEMI (Politic Analist)*
49. Kaveh FOULADI (Scholar)
50. Hayadeh FOULAD-POUR (Scholar)
51. Majid GHADIR (Artist)
52. Kambiz GHAEM-MAGHAM (Actor/Computer Analyst)
53. Maryam GHAFFARI (Archeologist)*
54. Shahyar GHANBARI (Poet/Vocalist)
55. Jamshid GOLMAKANI (Film-maker)
56. Mahmoud GOUDARZI (Journalist)
57. Safa HAERI (Journalist)*
58. Behzad HAFEZI (Journalist)
59. Mehdi HAJIJAFARI (Architect)
60. Ali-Asghar HAJ-SEYED JAVADI (Essayist)*
61. Ebrahim HARANDI (Poet/Scholar)
62. Avideh HASHEMI (Architect)
63. Hormoz HEKMAT (Scholar)
64. Daryoush HOMAYOON (Journalist)*
65. Fereydoun HOVEYDA (Writer)
66. Homayoun HOUSHYAR-NEJAD (Journalist)
67. Mohammad JAFARI (Actor)
68. Iraj JANATI-ATAYI (Poet/Playwright)*
69. Ramin KAMRAN (Sociologist)*
70. Parviz KARDAN (Actor/T.V. Director)*
71. Daryoush KARGAR (Writer)
72. Ahmad KARIMI-HAKAK (Scholar)*
73. Rafi KHACHATOURIAN (Actor)
74. Nasim KHAKSAR (Writer)*
75. Yahya KHAKZAD (Journalist)
76. Bijan KHALILI (Publisher)*
77. Mouloud KHANLARY (Essayist)*
78. Akbar KASHEFIAN (Writer)
79. Fereydoun KHAVAND (Scholar)*
80. Khosrow KHAZAIE (Scholar)
81. Abou KHERADMAND (Actress)*

82. Reza KHIYABANI (Writer)
83. Manouk KHODABAKHSHIAN (Essayist/T.V. Producer)
84. Esmail KHOEI (Poet)*
85. Lotfollah KHONJI (Commentator)
86. Morteza LATIFI (Journalist)
87. Ali LIMOUNADI (T.V. Director)
88. Amir MAENAVI (Journalist/Publisher)
89. Sousan MAFI (T.V. Reporter)
90. Mohammad-Houssein MAHINI (Film-maker)
91. Syrous MALAKOUTI (Composer)
92. Hossein MALEK (Scholar)*
93. Mehdi MEHRAMOUZ (Poet)
94. Daryoush MEHEGAN (Journalist)
95. Jamshid MESHKATI (Poet)
96. Morteza MIR AFTABI (Novelist)
97. Ahmad MIRFAKHRAIE (Scholar)
98. Ali MIRFETROSS (Scholar/Writer)
99. Mansour MOADDEL (Sociologist)
100. Hossein MOHRI (Journalist)*
101. Ardavan MOFID (Actor/Director)
102. Taghi MOKHTAR (Writer/Film-maker)
103. Taher MOMTAZ (Journalist)
104. Esfandiar MONFARED-ZADEH (Composer)*
105. Assadollah MOROVATI (Radio Producer)
106. Marva NABILI (Film-maker)
107. Mohsen NADERI-NEJAD (T.V. Programmer)*
108. Nader NADER-POUR (Poet)*
109. Firouzeh NADJI (Poet)
110. Niki NAZIE (Radio T.V. Producer)
111. Hassan NAZIEH (Lawyer)
112. Djamileh NEDAIE (Art Critic)
113. Javad NOURI (Journalist/Radio Programmer)
114. Partow NOURIALA (Poet)*
115. Ali-Reza NOURI-ZADEH (Poet/Commentator)
116. Kamran NOZAD (Actor)
117. Mahmoud OSTAD-MOHAMMAD (Dramatist)*
118. Yavar OSTOWAR/KAVIR (Poet)
119. Abbas PAHLAVAN (Writer)
120. Younes PARSABENAB (Scholar)

121. Koushiar PARSI (Writer)
122. Daryoush PIRNIA (Scholar)
123. Mansoureh PIRNIA (Journalist)
124. Ali POURTASH (Actor)
125. Iraj RAHMANI (Poet)
126. Hassan RAJAB-POUR (Journalist)
127. Zohreh RAMSEY (Actress)
128. Manouchehr RAZMARA (Physician)*
129. Morteza REZVANI (Writer)
130. Assad ROKHSARIAN (Poet)
131. Noushin SABETI (School administrator)
132. Parisa SAED (T.V. Programmer)
133. Morteza SAGHAFIAN (Poet)
134. Hassan SAHELNESHIN (Poet)
135. Ali SAJJADI (Journalist)
136. Kourosh SALEHI (Artist)
137. Satar SALIMI (Archealogist)
138. Hossein SAMAKAR (Writer)
139. Homa SARSHAR (Journalist)*
140. Hassan SATTARIAN (Scholar)
141. Parviz SAYYAD (Playwright/Film-maker)*
142. Massoud SEFATIAN (Architect)
143. Ali-Reza SEPASI (Writer/Publisher)
144. Shojaeldine SHAFA (Writer)*
145. Kamran SHAHGALDI (Administrator)
146. Cyrus SHARAFSHAHI (Journalist)
147. Ali SHARIFIAN (Reporter)
148. Behrouz SOURESRAFIL (Journalist)*
149. Djalal SOUSSAN-ABADI (Miniaturist)*
150. Syrous TABARESTANI (Writer/Scholar)
151. Farzaneh TAEIDI (Actress)
152. Barbad TAHERI (Cinematagropher)*
153. Nasser TAHMASEBI (Physician/Writer)
154. Hassan TEHRANCHIAN (Scholar)*
155. Shahram TEHRANI (Architect)
156. Fereydoun TONEKABONI (Writer)
157. Shadab VAJDI (Poet)
158. Houshang VAZIRI (Journalist)*
159. Ileen VEEGEN (Actress)

160. Mehdi YOUSEFI (Scholar/Dentist)
161. Hassan ZEREHI (Journalist)*
162. Akbar ZOLGHARNEIN (Poet)

APPENDIX B
UNIVERSITY ENTRANCE EXAMINATIONS

The following three student testimonies relate to the *concours* or university entrance examinations administered in the years 1981, 1982, 1983 and 1984. Over the years, the government's character investigations became progressively more systemic and organized. Persons as diverse as school principals, neighbors, members of the Islamic Association of Students, and representatives of local mosques are called upon to inform the government of the characters of prospective students. The government has on occasion implemented its character test through manipulation of entrance examinations. Reports from Iran, however, suggest that since 1985 the government has loosened its character selection process for undergraduate degrees while keeping it in place for graduate and post-graduate studies. Also, there is now a grievance procedure in place such that students can inquire about their *concours* ranking and contest the results of the government's character investigations. This partial loosening in the government's procedures can be attributed to the significant public criticism and to the government's recognition of Iran's need for its most talented and educated youth.

Middle East Watch took these testimonies from Iranians in exile and has changed their names at their request.

CASE OF MARYAM
CONCOURS EXAMINATION OF 1981

Maryam was among the first group of students to attend university in Iran after the revolution in the field of medicine, and also among the first to be "purged" on the basis of her family history. At the time, the government had not yet developed a system for character investigations before entrance into university, and the process took a more haphazard form after entrance.

In the spring of 1980, Maryam obtained her high school diploma and in the fall, universities were closed abruptly for an indefinite period to implement the "cultural revolution." Classes in preparation for university entrance examinations, however, continued during this time and Maryam was required to supplement her pre-revolutionary education with an in-depth study of the Koran, Ayatollah Khomeini's *Tozih al Masa'el* (Explanation of Problems), and Imam Ali's *Nahj al-Balagha* (Road to Eloquence). State-affiliated newspapers "advised" that voluntary work at hospitals would enhance a student's chance of attending university.

Maryam volunteered full time at the Hazrath-e Fatemeh Jadid Hospital for a year and a half, assisting primarily with the injured from the Iran-Iraq war.

Medical programs at universities were among the first to be reopened in response to the immediate needs of the war. The first set of *concours* examinations after the revolution was administered in the summer of 1981. Maryam took the examination for entrance into *Daneshgah-e Melli* (National University). In customary fashion, the names of persons who had passed the examination were posted on university walls, and her name was included among them. She started attending university in the fall of 1981.

After completion of her first semester, the officials at the university announced that "there had been mistakes in the grading of the first set of *concours* examinations and that it was necessary to interview every student on an individual basis." Maryam recalls that her father tried to dissuade her from attending the interview and recommended that she withdraw from university: "I was afraid. I didn't know what they would do to me if I said the wrong thing."

Maryam nevertheless decided to attend the interview. On the designated day, she appeared at the interview location. An armed revolutionary guard led her through a series of hallways to a large empty room where only a bearded man was seated behind a desk with files of paper. She was given an application to complete. The application asked for the name and occupation of her parents and the address of their home. She recalls the brief conversation that followed the completion of the application:

Question: Your father is a retired officer?
Response: Yes.
Q: When did he retire?
R: In 1981.
Q: Who decorated your father, the Shah?
R: Yes.
Q: You live in uptown Tehran?
R: Yes.
Q: Thank you. We will notify you of the results.

In a few weeks time, a modified list appeared on the walls of the university indicating those who had passed the entrance examination. This time Maryam's name was not among them.

Maryam left Iran in 1985 to continue her studies abroad.

Case of Sarah
Concours Examination of 1982

Upon completion of the "cultural revolution," the first nation-wide *concours* examinations were administered in 1982. Compared to the previous year, in which the exam had been administered to only medical students, the government had now fine-tuned its character test for university applicants so as to purge "undesirable" students before the commencement of their studies. Sarah was one of the students rejected as a result of this test.

The *concours* exam was administered in two stages. In order to attend the second stage of the exam, it was necessary for the student to have passed the first stage as well as the character test. Students submitted a list of references to the authorities who could vouch for their character. This list often included teachers, neighbors, friends, high school principal and representatives from the local mosque. Once the student had passed the first stage, government officials would make character inquires and notify the student whether he or she should take the second half of the exam.

Sarah's list only had the names of neighbors and friends. When Sarah had gone to her high school to get her report card, her principal had told her, "Don't even try to get on the list [of approved students]." Sarah's references were contacted by the government, indicating that she had passed the first part of the exam, but she was never notified by the government to take the second part.

Sarah recalls, "There was no recourse. Nowhere to make inquires." She also recalls, "There was much public criticism of these methods."

Sarah left Iran in 1991, and is continuing her studies abroad.

Case of Leila
Concours Examinations of 1983 and of 1984

Leila took the concours in 1983 and 1984. The first year, she was rejected on character grounds, although she had ranked high enough for admission into her profession of choice, medicine. The second year, she was accepted into her last choice, midwifery. Leila's problems with the authorities were confounded by the fact that she is from a small town in the north of Iran, as she states, "where everyone knows everyone."

Leila graduated from high school in 1983. That year, the principal of the school had been replaced by a "religious" woman. Leila was always a straight A student but this year she was given a lower grade for *Enzebat Eslami* (Islamic Discipline). When she approached her principal about her discipline grade, the principal stated, "the times that you received an A have passed."

Leila took the *concours* in 1983, administered in two stages. After the first stage, her name was published in the newspapers among those who had passed. Leila used her first eleven choices for medicine, which is one of the most difficult fields to enter, and her last choice for medical technology, one of the easier fields to enter.[1] She took the second part of the exam, but this time her name was not printed in the newspaper.

Leila recalls, "I was shocked that I had even failed medical technology. Her family, thinking that she had not prepared herself well enough, urged her to attend *concours* preparation courses and to take the exam once again. Leila came to Tehran to attend the preparation courses.

Leila remembers well the day, about two months before the 1984 exam, when she overheard a group of fellow students at the preparation course discussing reports they had received from the government indicating their ranking in the *concours* in terms of every profession they had selected as well as the cut-off point for that profession. "I was very surprised," Leila states, "I had never received any such report." Upon inquiring about this report, she was told by one of the students, "Promise you will not be upset. They send these cards only to people who have passed *Tahgeegh* (Investigation)."

---

[1] Students are given twelve choices to indicate preferred professions. Every profession has ranking and quota prerequisites. A student's admittance to the profession depends on his or her ranking in the exam.

Leila inquired at the Ministry of Culture and Higher Education in Tehran about the report she had never received. "First, the official remarked how I did not look like I would have failed (I was dressed in full compliance with Islamic principles) and then he sent me to a board where the names of persons who had mistakenly not recieved the report were posted," Leila states. Since she did not find her name there, the official stated "then you must have failed the investigation." I asked him if he could nevertheless look up my grades and tell me if I had scored high enough for medicine. "He returned with a sad face," Leila recalls, "and said that I had ranked much higher than medical technology [required] but that he couldn't say more." Since all of Leila's other choices were medicine, this meant that her grades had been high enough for acceptance into medicine. "This discovery was very disheartening, especially two months prior to the next round of exams," she states.

She was urged to clear up her investigation file before taking the exam again. She returned to her home town to get character approval letters. When she asked her principal for a letter, she was told, "At prayer time, you would not pray with the other girls and instead would eat a sandwich." When she approached the *Anjoman-Eslami Daneshjuyan* (Islamic Association of Students) at her school, she was told, "You had Tudeh [Communist] friends." (In this regard, Leila states, "A student my age determined my destiny.") When her father approached the Islamic council at the local mosque, he was told, "the vote within the council at the time your daughter had applied for university was three for and two against. The complaint was that your family did not go to mosque."

She nevertheless took the next round of entrance examinations in 1984. She once again used her first eleven options for medicine and the last for midwifery. This year, the government notified her of her ranking, and she was told that she could either enter midwifery or the profession she had selected the previous year, medical technology. She entered midwifery, which requires two and a half years of study.

In conclusion, Leila stated, "I will never forgive them for changing the course of my life in this way." She has now resumed her studies abroad in a different field.